GRILLING
COOKBOOK

Publications International, Ltd.

Microwave Cooking: Microwave ovens vary in wattage. Use the cooking times as guidelines and check for doneness before adding more time.

WARNING: Food preparation, baking and cooking involve inherent dangers: misuse of electric products, sharp electric tools, boiling water, hot stoves, allergic reactions, foodborne illnesses and the like, pose numerous potential risks. Publications International, Ltd. (PIL) assumes no responsibility or liability for any damages you may experience as a result of following recipes, instructions, tips or advice in this publication.

While we hope this publication helps you find new ways to eat delicious foods, you may not always achieve the results desired due to variations in ingredients, cooking temperatures, typos, errors, omissions or individual cooking abilities.

Let's get social!
@Publications_International
@PublicationsInternational
www.pilbooks.com

CONTENTS

GRILLED CLASSICS

CHIPOTLE SPICE-RUBBED BEER CAN CHICKEN

MAKES 4 SERVINGS

- 2 tablespoons packed brown sugar
- 2 teaspoons smoked paprika
- 2 teaspoons ground cumin
- 1 teaspoon salt
- 1 teaspoon garlic powder
- 1 teaspoon chili powder
- ½ teaspoon ground chipotle pepper
- 1 whole chicken (3½ to 4 pounds), rinsed and patted dry
- 1 can (12 ounces) beer

1. Prepare grill for indirect cooking over medium heat. Lightly oil grid.

2. Combine brown sugar, paprika, cumin, salt, garlic powder, chili powder and chipotle pepper in small bowl; stir to blend. Gently loosen skin of chicken over breast, legs and thighs. Rub sugar mixture under and over skin and inside cavity. Discard one fourth of beer. Hold chicken upright with cavity pointing down; insert beer can into cavity.

3. Place chicken on grid, standing upright on can. Spread legs slightly for support. Grill, covered, 1 hour 15 minutes or until chicken is cooked through (165°F).

4. Lift chicken off beer can using metal tongs. Let rest upright on large cutting board 5 minutes before carving.

WESTERN BARBECUE BURGERS WITH BEER BARBECUE SAUCE

MAKES 4 SERVINGS

1½ pounds ground beef

1 cup smokehouse-style barbecue sauce

¼ cup brown ale

½ teaspoon salt

¼ teaspoon black pepper

1 red onion, cut into ½-inch-thick slices

4 hamburger buns

8 slices thick-cut bacon, crisp-cooked

Tomato slices

Lettuce leaves

1. Prepare grill for direct cooking over medium-high heat. Lightly oil grid. Shape beef into four patties about ¾ inch thick.

2. Combine barbecue sauce, ale, salt and pepper in small saucepan. Bring to a boil; boil 1 minute. Set aside.

3. Grill burgers, covered, 8 to 10 minutes or to desired doneness, turning occasionally. Grill onion 4 minutes or until softened and slightly charred, turning occasionally.

4. Serve burgers on buns with onion, bacon, barbecue sauce mixture, tomatoes and lettuce.

CLASSIC BABY BACK RIBS ▶

MAKES ABOUT 4 SERVINGS

3 to 4 pounds pork baby back ribs, cut into 3-rib portions (2 to 3 racks)

1 cup *Cattlemen's*® Award Winning Classic Barbecue Sauce

1. Grill ribs over indirect heat on a covered grill for 1½ hours (or in a 350°F oven).

2. Baste with barbecue sauce. Cook 30 minutes longer until meat is very tender. Serve with additional barbecue sauce.

TIP

To make Blazin' BBQ Wings, mix equal amounts *Cattlemen's*® Award Winning Classic Barbecue Sauce with *Frank's*® *Redhot*® Original Cayenne Pepper Sauce and coat cooked wings.

ZESTY STEAK FAJITAS

MAKES 4 SERVINGS

¾ cup FRENCH'S® Worcestershire Sauce, divided

1 pound boneless top round, sirloin or flank steak

3 tablespoons taco seasoning mix

2 red or green bell peppers, cut into quarters

1 to 2 large onions, cut into thick slices

¾ cup chili sauce

8 (8-inch) flour or corn tortillas, heated

Sour cream and shredded cheese (optional)

1. Pour ½ cup Worcestershire over steak in deep dish. Cover and refrigerate 30 minutes or up to 3 hours. Drain meat and rub both sides with seasoning mix. Discard marinade.

2. Grill meat and vegetables over medium-hot coals 10 to 15 minutes until meat is medium rare and vegetables are charred, but tender.

3. Thinly slice meat and vegetables. Place in large bowl. Add chili sauce and remaining ¼ cup Worcestershire. Toss to coat. Serve in tortillas and garnish with sour cream and cheese.

ALL-AMERICAN BARBECUE GRILLED CHICKEN

MAKES 4 SERVINGS

1 sheet REYNOLDS WRAP® Non-Stick Foil

6 chicken pieces

1 cup Southwestern Barbecue Sauce

HEAT grill to medium-high. Make drainage holes in sheet of REYNOLDS WRAP® Non-Stick Foil with a large fork. Place foil sheet on grill grate with non-stick (dull) side facing up; immediately place chicken on foil.

GRILL covered 10 minutes. Turn chicken; brush chicken with barbecue sauce. Grill 10 minutes longer; turn chicken. Brush again with barbecue sauce; continue grilling until chicken is tender and reaches 180°F. Discard any remaining sauce.

SOUTHWESTERN BARBECUE SAUCE

Add 2 teaspoons chili powder, 1 teaspoon dry mustard, ¼ teaspoon garlic powder and ¼ teaspoon cayenne pepper to barbecue sauce. Grill as directed above.

GUACAMOLE BURGERS

MAKES 4 SERVINGS

1 small avocado

2 tablespoons finely chopped tomato

1 tablespoon chopped fresh cilantro

2 teaspoons lime juice, divided

1 teaspoon minced jalapeño pepper

¼ teaspoon salt, divided

2 tablespoons sour cream

2 tablespoons mayonnaise

½ teaspoon ground cumin

4 teaspoons vegetable oil, divided

1 medium onion, cut into thin slices

1 small green bell pepper, cut into thin slices

1 small red bell pepper, cut into thin slices

1¼ pounds ground beef

Salt and black pepper

4 slices Monterey Jack cheese

4 hamburger buns, split and toasted

1 can (4 ounces) diced fire-roasted jalapeño peppers, drained

1. Mash avocado in medium bowl. Stir in tomato, cilantro, 1 teaspoon lime juice, minced jalapeño and ⅛ teaspoon salt; mix well. Cover; refrigerate until ready to use. Combine sour cream, mayonnaise, remaining 1 teaspoon lime juice and cumin in small bowl; stir to blend. Cover; refrigerate until ready to use.

2. Heat 2 teaspoons oil in large skillet over medium-high heat. Add onion; cook 8 minutes or until onion is very tender and begins to turn golden, stirring occasionally. (Add a few teaspoons water to skillet if onion begins to burn.) Remove to bowl.

3. Meanwhile, prepare grill for direct cooking over medium-high heat. Lightly oil grid.

4. Add remaining 2 teaspoons oil to skillet. Add bell peppers; cook and stir 5 minutes or until tender. Remove to bowl with onion; season vegetables with remaining ⅛ teaspoon salt.

5. Shape beef into four 5-inch patties; sprinkle both sides generously with salt and black pepper. Grill patties about 5 minutes per side or until cooked through (160°F). Top patties with cheese slices during last minute of cooking.

6. Spread sour cream mixture over bottom halves of buns. Top with vegetables, burgers, guacamole, fire-roasted jalapeños and top halves of buns.

GRILLED FAJITAS

MAKES 4 SERVINGS

- 1 cup WISH-BONE® Robusto Italian or Italian Dressing
- 1 Tbsp. fresh lime juice
- 2 Tbsp. finely chopped fresh cilantro
- 1 Tbsp. grated lime peel
- 1 lb. boneless beef top round sirloin steak or boneless, skinless chicken breasts, cut into 1-inch cubes
- 1 large red and/or green bell pepper, cut into large chunks
- 2 medium red or yellow onions, quartered
- Flour tortillas, warmed
- Fajita Fixin's: Shredded cheese, chopped tomatoes, sour cream, shredded lettuce and/or guacamole

1. Blend WISH-BONE® Robusto Italian Dressing, lime juice, cilantro and lime peel. Pour ¾ cup marinade over steak, bell pepper and onions in large, shallow nonaluminum baking dish or resealable plastic bag; turn to coat. Cover, or close bag, and marinate in refrigerator, turning occasionally, up to 3 hours. Refrigerate remaining marinade.

2. Remove steak and vegetables from marinade, discarding marinade. Alternately thread steak and vegetables on skewers.* Grill or broil, turning and brushing occasionally with refrigerated marinade, until steak is desired doneness and vegetables are tender.

3. Fold tortilla around skewer and gently pull steak and vegetables off skewer into tortilla. Garnish with Fajita Fixin's.

If using wooden skewers, soak at least 30 minutes prior to use to avoid burning.

TIP

If you want to serve moist, delicious corn on the cob, brush on HELLMANN'S® or BEST FOODS® Real Mayonnaise before grilling.

GRILLED CHICKEN WITH CORN AND BLACK BEAN SALSA

MAKES 4 SERVINGS

½ cup corn

½ cup finely chopped red bell pepper

½ of a 15-ounce can black beans, rinsed and drained

½ ripe medium avocado, diced

¼ cup chopped fresh cilantro

2 tablespoons fresh lime juice

1 tablespoon chopped pickled jalapeño pepper

½ teaspoon salt, divided

1 teaspoon black pepper

½ teaspoon chili powder

4 boneless skinless chicken breasts (4 ounces each), pounded to ½-inch thickness

1. Combine corn, bell pepper, beans, avocado, cilantro, lime juice, jalapeño and ¼ teaspoon salt in medium bowl. Set aside.

2. Combine black pepper, remaining ¼ teaspoon salt and chili powder in small bowl; sprinkle over chicken.

3. Coat grill pan with nonstick cooking spray. Cook chicken over medium-high heat 4 minutes per side or until no longer pink in center.

4. Serve chicken topped with half of salsa; refrigerate remaining salsa for another use.

RIB EYE STEAKS WITH CHILI BUTTER ▶

MAKES 4 SERVINGS

½ cup (1 stick) butter, softened

2 teaspoons chili powder

1 teaspoon minced garlic

1 teaspoon Dijon mustard

⅛ teaspoon ground red pepper or chipotle chile pepper

4 beef rib eye steaks

Salt and black pepper

1. Combine butter, chili powder, garlic, mustard and red pepper in medium bowl; stir until smooth. Place mixture on sheet of waxed paper. Roll mixture back and forth into 6-inch log using waxed paper. If butter is too soft, refrigerate up to 30 minutes. Wrap with waxed paper; refrigerate at least 1 hour or up to 2 days.

2. Prepare grill for direct cooking over medium-high heat. Lightly oil grid. Season steaks with salt and black pepper.

3. Grill steaks, covered, 8 to 10 minutes or until desired doneness, turning occasionally. Slice chili butter; serve with steak.

BARBECUE CHICKEN WINGS

MAKES 4 SERVINGS

4 pounds chicken wings (about 16 to 20 wings)

Salt and black pepper

¼ cup chopped onion

2 tablespoons olive oil

2 cloves garlic minced

1½ cups prepared barbecue sauce

1. Prepare grill for direct cooking over medium-high heat. Lightly oil grid. Season chicken with salt and black pepper.

2. Place onion, oil and garlic in medium microwavable bowl. Microwave on HIGH 1½ to 2 minutes or until onion is tender. Add barbecue sauce; stir until blended. Set aside.

3. Place chicken on grid. Grill, covered, 25 minutes or until chicken is no longer pink and juices run clear, turning after 15 minutes. Serve with barbecue sauce mixture.

CHEDDAR-BEER BURGERS WITH BACON

MAKES 4 SERVINGS

1½ pounds ground beef

4 ounces sharp Cheddar cheese, cut into ½-inch cubes

½ cup beer

¼ cup chopped fresh parsley

1 teaspoon paprika

¾ teaspoon garlic powder

¾ teaspoon salt

¼ teaspoon black pepper

¼ cup ketchup

2 tablespoons mayonnaise

4 hamburger buns

4 lettuce leaves

4 slices tomato

4 thick slices red onion

8 slices bacon, cooked

1. Prepare grill for direct cooking over medium-high heat. Lightly oil grid.

2. Combine beef, cheese, beer, parsley, paprika, garlic powder, salt and pepper in large bowl; stir to blend. Shape into four patties, making centers of patties slightly thinner than edges.

3. Grill patties, covered, 8 to 10 minutes (or uncovered, 13 to 15 minutes) to medium (160°F) or to desired doneness, turning once.

4. Meanwhile, combine ketchup and mayonnaise in small bowl. Top bottom half of each bun with ketchup mixture, lettuce, tomato, onion, burger and bacon; cover with top halves of buns.

SWEET 'N' SPICY GRILLED SHRIMP

MAKES 4 SERVINGS

REYNOLDS WRAP®
Non-Stick Foil

½ **cup cocktail sauce**

1 **tablespoon plus
2 teaspoons seafood
seasoning, divided**

1 **teaspoon garlic powder**

1 **pound medium raw
shrimp, peeled and
deveined**

1 **teaspoon garlic powder**

2 **teaspoons packed
brown sugar**

COMBINE cocktail sauce, 2 teaspoons seafood seasoning and garlic powder. Cover and reserve for dipping sauce.

PLACE shrimp in a medium bowl. Sprinkle remaining ingredients over shrimp. Stir gently to coat shrimp evenly.

PREHEAT grill to medium-high. Make drainage holes in a sheet of REYNOLDS WRAP® Non-Stick Foil with a large fork. Place foil on grill grate with non-stick (dull) side facing up. Immediately arrange shrimp in a single layer on foil.

GRILL 4 to 6 minutes in covered grill, turning once, until shrimp are firm and pink. Serve shrimp with dipping sauce.

BUFFALO SLIDERS ▶

MAKES 6 SERVINGS

1½ pounds ground beef

½ cup finely chopped bell pepper

3 tablespoons any flavor **FRANK'S® RedHot®** Buffalo Wings Sauce

12 mini slider buns or dinner rolls

Lettuce and shredded cheese

1. Mix beef, bell pepper and **FRANK'S RedHot** Buffalo Wings Sauce; shape into 12 mini patties.

2. Grill or broil sliders until desired doneness, turning once.

3. Serve sliders on rolls with lettuce and cheese.

GRILLED GARLIC-PEPPER SHRIMP

MAKES 4 SERVINGS

⅓ cup olive oil

2 tablespoons lemon juice

1 teaspoon garlic-pepper seasoning

20 jumbo raw shrimp, peeled and deveined

Lemon wedges (optional)

1. Combine oil, lemon juice and seasoning in large resealable food storage bag; add shrimp. Marinate 20 to 30 minutes in refrigerator, turning bag once.

2. Prepare grill for direct cooking over medium heat. Lightly oil grid.

3. Thread 5 shrimp onto each of 4 skewers;* discard marinade. Grill 6 minutes or until pink and opaque. Serve with lemon wedges, if desired.

If using wooden skewers, soak in water at least 20 minutes before using to prevent scorching.

BRATWURST SANDWICHES

MAKES 4 SERVINGS

4 bratwurst (about
  1 pound)

1 bottle or can
  (12 ounces) beer

1 onion, sliced

1 red bell pepper, cut into
  thin strips

1 green bell pepper, cut
  into thin strips

1 tablespoon olive oil

¾ teaspoon salt

½ teaspoon black pepper

4 hoagie or submarine
  sandwich rolls, split

  Spicy brown or Dijon
  mustard

  Hot sport peppers
  (optional)

1. Combine bratwurst and beer in medium saucepan; bring to a boil over high heat. Reduce heat to low. Simmer, uncovered, 20 to 25 minutes or until bratwurst are no longer pink in center, turning occasionally. Cool in liquid. Drain bratwurst; wrap in foil or resealable food storage bag. Refrigerate up to 24 hours.

2. Combine onion and bell peppers on large sheet of heavy-duty foil. Drizzle with oil; season with salt and black pepper. Place another sheet of foil over vegetables; fold up all edges of foil, forming packet. Refrigerate up to 24 hours.

3. Prepare grill for direct cooking over medium-high heat. Lightly oil grid. Place foil packet on grid; grill 5 minutes. Place bratwurst on grid; turn vegetable packet over. Continue grilling 10 minutes or until bratwurst are heated through and vegetables are tender, turning bratwurst and foil packet once.

4. Place rolls, split sides down, on grid to toast lightly during final minutes of grilling. Serve bratwurst and vegetables in rolls. Serve with mustard and hot peppers, if desired.

GRILLED SKIRT STEAK FAJITAS

MAKES 4 SERVINGS

- 1½ **pounds skirt steak**
- ½ **cup pale ale**
- 3 **tablespoons lime juice**
- 1 **teaspoon ground cumin**
- 2 **tablespoons olive oil**
- 1 **cup thinly sliced red onion**
- 1 **cup thinly sliced red and green bell peppers**
- 2 **cloves garlic, minced**
- 3 **plum tomatoes, each cut into 4 wedges**
- 1 **tablespoon soy sauce**
- ¾ **teaspoon salt**
- ¼ **teaspoon black pepper**
- 8 **(7-inch) flour tortillas, warmed**
  Lime wedges (optional)

1. Place steak in large resealable food storage bag. Combine ale, lime juice and cumin in small bowl; pour over steak. Seal bag; turn to coat. Refrigerate 2 hours, turning occasionally.

2. Heat oil in large nonstick skillet over medium-high heat. Add onion; cook and stir 2 to 3 minutes or until beginning to soften. Add bell peppers; cook and stir 7 to 8 minutes or until softened. Add garlic; cook and stir 1 minute. Add tomatoes; cook 2 minutes or just until beginning to soften. Add soy sauce; cook 1 minute. Keep warm.

3. Prepare grill for direct cooking over medium-high heat. Lightly oil grid.

4. Remove steak from marinade; discard marinade. Sprinkle with salt and black pepper. Grill 4 to 6 minutes on each side to 145°F or desired doneness. Remove to large cutting board; cut across grain into ¼-inch-thick slices. Serve steak and vegetable mixture in tortillas. Serve with lime wedges, if desired.

KOREAN BEEF SHORT RIBS

MAKES 4 TO 6 SERVINGS

2½ pounds beef chuck flanken-style short ribs, cut ⅜ to ½ inch thick*

¼ cup chopped green onions

¼ cup water

¼ cup soy sauce

1 tablespoon sugar

2 teaspoons grated fresh ginger

2 teaspoons dark sesame oil

2 cloves garlic, minced

½ teaspoon black pepper

1 tablespoon sesame seeds, toasted**

*Flanken-style ribs can be ordered from your butcher. They are cross-cut short ribs sawed through the bones.

**To toast sesame seeds, spread seeds in small skillet. Shake skillet over medium-low heat 3 minutes or until seeds begin to pop and turn golden.

1. Place ribs in large resealable food storage bag. Combine green onions, water, soy sauce, sugar, ginger, oil, garlic and pepper in small bowl; stir to blend. Pour over ribs. Seal bag; turn to coat. Marinate in refrigerator at least 4 hours or up to 8 hours, turning occasionally.

2. Prepare grill for direct cooking over medium-high heat. Lightly oil grid. Remove ribs from marinade; reserve marinade. Grill ribs, covered, 5 minutes. Brush lightly with reserved marinade; turn and brush again. Discard remaining marinade. Continue to grill, covered, 5 to 6 minutes for medium (165°F) or to desired doneness. Sprinkle with sesame seeds.

BACKYARD BARBECUE BURGERS

MAKES 6 SERVINGS

1½ pounds ground beef

5 tablespoons barbecue sauce, divided

1 onion, cut into thick slices

1 tomato, sliced

2 tablespoons olive oil

6 Kaiser rolls, split

6 leaves green or red leaf lettuce

1. Prepare grill for direct cooking over medium-high heat. Lightly oil grid. Combine beef and 2 tablespoons barbecue sauce in large bowl. Shape into 6 (1-inch-thick) patties.

2. Grill patties, covered, 8 to 10 minutes (or uncovered 13 to 15 minutes) to medium (160°F) or to desired doneness, turning occasionally. Brush both sides with remaining 3 tablespoons barbecue sauce during last 5 minutes of cooking.

3. Meanwhile, brush onion* and tomato slices with oil. Grill onion slices about 10 minutes and tomato slices 2 to 3 minutes.

4. Just before serving, place rolls, cut side down, on grid; grill until lightly toasted. Serve burgers on rolls with tomato, onion and lettuce.

*Onion slices may be cooked on the stovetop. Heat 2 tablespoons oil in large skillet over medium heat; add onions and cook 10 minutes or until tender and slightly browned, stirring frequently.

PERFECT POULTRY

SPICED CHICKEN SKEWERS WITH YOGURT-TAHINI SAUCE

MAKES 8 SERVINGS

1 cup plain nonfat or regular Greek yogurt

¼ cup chopped fresh parsley, plus additional for garnish

¼ cup tahini

2 tablespoons lemon juice

1 clove garlic

¾ teaspoon salt, divided

1 tablespoon vegetable oil

2 teaspoons garam masala

1 pound boneless skinless chicken breasts, cut into 1-inch pieces

1. Prepare grill for direct cooking over medium-high heat. Lightly oil grid.

2. For sauce, combine yogurt, ¼ cup parsley, tahini, lemon juice, garlic and ¼ teaspoon salt in food processor or blender; process until smooth. Set aside.

3. Combine oil, garam masala and remaining ½ teaspoon salt in medium bowl; stir to blend. Add chicken; toss to coat. Thread chicken on eight 6-inch wooden or metal skewers.*

4. Grill chicken skewers 5 minutes per side or until chicken is no longer pink. Serve with sauce. Garnish with additional parsley.

If using wooden skewers, soak in cold water 20 to 30 minutes to prevent burning.

JAMAICAN RUM CHICKEN

MAKES 6 SERVINGS

½ cup dark rum

2 tablespoons packed brown sugar

2 tablespoons lime juice or lemon juice

2 tablespoons soy sauce

4 cloves garlic, minced

1 to 2 jalapeño peppers, seeded and minced

1 tablespoon minced fresh ginger

1 teaspoon dried thyme

½ teaspoon black pepper

6 boneless skinless chicken breasts

1. To prepare marinade, combine rum, brown sugar, lime juice, soy sauce, garlic, jalapeños, ginger, thyme and black pepper in glass measuring cup. Place chicken in large resealable food storage bag; pour marinade over chicken. Seal bag; turn to coat. Refrigerate 4 hours or overnight, turning bag once or twice.

2. Prepare grill for direct cooking over medium heat. Lightly oil grid.

3. Drain chicken; reserve marinade. Grill, covered, 10 to 14 minutes or until chicken is no longer pink in center, turning once.

4. Meanwhile, bring remaining marinade to a boil in small saucepan. Boil 5 minutes or until marinade is reduced by about half. To serve, drizzle marinade over chicken.

CHICKEN BURRITO BOWLS

MAKES 4 SERVINGS

3 cloves garlic

½ medium red onion, coarsely chopped

2 tablespoons olive oil

1½ tablespoons adobo sauce (from small can of chipotle peppers in adobo)

1 tablespoon ancho chili powder

1½ teaspoons ground cumin

1 teaspoon salt

1 teaspoon dried oregano

½ teaspoon black pepper

½ cup water

1 pound boneless skinless chicken thighs

1⅓ cups cooked black beans

3 cups cooked white or brown rice

Optional toppings: guacamole, salsa, corn and/or shredded lettuce with sliced green onions and chopped fresh tomato

1. With motor running, drop garlic cloves through feed tube of food processor; process until garlic is finely chopped. Add onion, oil, adobo sauce, chili powder, cumin, salt, oregano and black pepper; process until well blended. Add water; process until smooth.

2. Place chicken in large resealable food storage bag. Add marinade; seal bag and turn to coat. Refrigerate at least 3 hours or overnight.

3. Remove chicken from refrigerator about 30 minutes before cooking. Prepare grill for direct cooking over medium-high heat. Lightly oil grid.

4. Grill chicken 6 minutes per side or until cooked through (165°F). Remove to large plate; tent with foil. Let stand 10 minutes before chopping into ½-inch pieces.

5. Serve chicken and beans over rice with desired toppings.

GRILLED CHICKEN WITH SOUTHERN BARBECUE SAUCE

MAKES 6 SERVINGS

½ cup chopped onion (about 1 small)

4 cloves garlic, minced

1 can (16 ounces) tomato sauce

¾ cup water

3 tablespoons packed light brown sugar

3 tablespoons chili sauce

2 teaspoons chili powder

2 teaspoons dried thyme

2 teaspoons Worcestershire sauce

¾ teaspoon ground red pepper

½ teaspoon ground cinnamon

½ teaspoon black pepper

6 boneless skinless chicken breasts (2¼ pounds)

1. Spray medium skillet with nonstick cooking spray; heat over medium heat. Add onion and garlic; cook and stir 5 minutes or until tender.

2. Stir in tomato sauce, water, brown sugar, chili sauce, chili powder, thyme, Worcestershire sauce, red pepper, cinnamon and black pepper; bring to a boil. Reduce heat to low. Simmer, uncovered, 30 minutes or until mixture is reduced to about 1½ cups. Reserve ¾ cup sauce for basting.

3. Meanwhile, prepare grill for indirect cooking over medium heat. Lightly oil grid.

4. Grill chicken, covered, 40 to 45 minutes or until cooked through (165°F), turning chicken several times and basting occasionally with reserved sauce. Heat remaining sauce in same skillet over medium heat; spoon over chicken.

CAJUN BBQ BEER CAN CHICKEN

MAKES 12 SERVINGS

4 (12-ounce) cans beer or non-alcoholic malt beverage

1½ cups *Cattlemen's®* Award Winning Classic Barbecue Sauce

¾ cup Cajun spice or Southwest seasoning blend

3 whole chickens (3 to 4 pounds each)

12 sprigs fresh thyme

CAJUN BBQ SAUCE

1 cup *Cattlemen's®* Award Winning Classic Barbecue Sauce

½ cup beer or non-alcoholic malt beverage

¼ cup butter

1 tablespoon Cajun spice or Southwest seasoning blend

1. Combine 1 can beer, 1½ cups barbecue sauce and ½ cup spice blend. Following manufacturer's instructions, fill marinade injection needle with marinade. Inject chickens in several places at least 1-inch deep. Place chickens into resealable plastic food storage bags. Pour any remaining marinade over chickens. Seal bag; marinate in refrigerator 1 to 3 hours or overnight.

2. Meanwhile, prepare Cajun BBQ Sauce: In saucepan, combine 1 cup barbecue sauce, ½ cup beer, butter and 1 tablespoon spice blend. Simmer 5 minutes. Refrigerate and warm just before serving.

3. Open remaining cans of beer. Spill out about ½ cup beer from each can. Using can opener, punch several holes in tops of cans. Spoon about 1 tablespoon additional spice blend and 4 sprigs thyme into each can. Place 1 can upright into each cavity of chicken, arranging legs forward so chicken stands upright.

4. Place chickens upright over indirect heat on barbecue grill. Cook on a covered grill on medium-high (350°F), about 1½ hours until thigh meat registers 180°F internal temperature. (Cover chickens with foil if they become too brown while cooking.) Let stand 10 minutes before serving. Using tongs, carefully remove cans from chicken. Cut into quarters to serve. Serve with Cajun BBQ Sauce.

SAN FRANCISCO GRILLED CHICKEN SANDWICHES

MAKES 2 SANDWICHES

2 boneless, skinless chicken breast halves

3 tablespoons Italian or ranch salad dressing

2 slices (2 ounces) SARGENTO® Deli Style Sliced Muenster or SARGENTO® Deli Style Sliced Swiss Cheese

2 kaiser rolls, split or 4 slices sourdough bread

8 spinach leaves

½ cup alfalfa sprouts

6 avocado slices

2 tablespoons thick salsa

1. Pound chicken breast halves to ¼-inch thickness. Place in shallow bowl; pour dressing over chicken. Cover; marinate in refrigerator 1 hour.

2. Drain chicken; discard dressing. Grill over medium coals 3 minutes; turn. Top each chicken breast half with cheese slice; continue to grill 2 minutes or until chicken is cooked through. On bottom half of each roll, layer half of the spinach leaves, sprouts and avocado slices. Top each sandwich with grilled chicken breast, half of salsa and top half of roll.

LIME-GRILLED CHICKEN WITH CHIVE POLENTA

MAKES 4 SERVINGS

1 tablespoon chopped
   fresh parsley

1 tablespoon olive oil

1 teaspoon minced garlic

1 teaspoon grated lime
   peel

3 cups chicken broth

¾ cup yellow cornmeal

¼ cup sour cream

2 tablespoons snipped
   fresh chives

4 boneless skinless
   chicken breasts

½ teaspoon salt

1 cup salsa

1. Combine parsley, oil, garlic and lime peel in small bowl; mix well. Set aside.

2. Bring broth to a boil in large saucepan. Gradually stir in cornmeal. Reduce heat to low. Cook and stir 15 minutes or until mixture is thick and pulls away from side of pan. (Mixture may be lumpy.) Stir in sour cream and chives; cover. Set aside and keep warm.

3. Prepare grill for direct cooking over medium-high heat. Lightly oil grid. Sprinkle chicken with salt.

4. Grill 5 to 7 minutes on each side or until no longer pink in center. Spread parsley mixture evenly over both sides of chicken; cook 1 minute on each side. Serve chicken with polenta; top with salsa.

GREEK CHICKEN BURGERS WITH CUCUMBER YOGURT SAUCE

MAKES 4 SERVINGS

½ cup plus 2 tablespoons plain nonfat Greek yogurt

½ medium cucumber, peeled, seeded and finely chopped

Juice of ½ lemon

3 cloves garlic, minced, divided

2 teaspoons finely chopped fresh mint *or* ½ teaspoon dried mint

⅛ teaspoon salt

⅛ teaspoon ground white pepper

1 pound ground chicken breast

¾ cup (3 ounces) crumbled feta cheese

4 large kalamata olives, rinsed, patted dry and minced

1 egg

½ to 1 teaspoon dried oregano

¼ teaspoon black pepper

Mixed baby lettuce (optional)

Fresh mint leaves (optional)

1. Combine yogurt, cucumber, lemon juice, 2 cloves garlic, 2 teaspoons chopped mint, salt and white pepper in medium bowl; mix well. Cover and refrigerate until ready to serve.

2. Prepare grill for direct cooking over medium-high heat. Lightly oil grid. Combine chicken, cheese, olives, egg, oregano, black pepper and remaining 1 clove garlic in large bowl; mix well. Shape mixture into four patties.

3. Grill patties 5 to 7 minutes per side or until cooked through (165°F).

4. Serve burgers with sauce and mixed greens, if desired. Garnish with mint leaves.

APRICOT COLA AND ROSEMARY CHICKEN

MAKES 4 SERVINGS

- 4 boneless skinless chicken breasts
- 2 cloves garlic, minced
- ¼ teaspoon kosher salt
- ¼ teaspoon red pepper flakes
- 4 tablespoons apricot preserves
- ½ cup cola beverage
- ¼ cup soy sauce
- 2 tablespoons chopped fresh rosemary, plus additional for garnish

1. Place chicken in large baking dish. Rub garlic, salt and red pepper flakes over chicken. Spread 1 tablespoon apricot preserves over each chicken breast. Drizzle with cola and soy sauce; sprinkle with 2 tablespoons rosemary. Cover and marinate at room temperature at least 30 minutes.

2. Prepare grill for direct cooking over medium-high heat. Lightly oil grid. Remove chicken from marinade; discard marinade.

3. Grill chicken 5 minutes per side or until chicken is cooked through. Garnish with additional rosemary.

GRILLED CUBAN PARTY SANDWICH

MAKES 6 SANDWICHES

¾ cup plus 1 to
   2 tablespoons
   olive oil, divided

6 tablespoons lime juice

4 cloves garlic, minced

2¼ teaspoons salt

¾ teaspoon black pepper

2 boneless skinless
   chicken breasts
   (about ½ pound),
   rinsed and patted dry

1 medium yellow onion

1 loaf ciabatta bread
   (1 pound), cut in half
   lengthwise

¼ cup chopped fresh
   cilantro

6 ounces fresh mozzarella,
   sliced

1 medium tomato, thinly
   sliced

1. For marinade, combine ¾ cup oil, lime juice, garlic, salt and pepper in medium bowl.

2. Pour ¼ cup of marinade into large resealable food storage bag. Add chicken breasts; coat well. Seal bag. Refrigerate up to 2 hours. Refrigerate remaining marinade.

3. Prepare grill for direct cooking over medium-high heat. Lightly oil grid. Cut onion horizontally into ½-inch-thick slices, leaving rings intact. Thread onion onto skewers.

4. Remove chicken from marinade; discard marinade. Grill chicken, uncovered, 12 to 15 minutes or until internal temperature reaches 160°F, turning halfway through cooking time. Meanwhile, brush onion with 1 tablespoon oil; place on grill beside chicken. Grill onion 8 to 12 minutes or until soft and browned, turning halfway through cooking time.

5. Remove chicken and onion to large cutting board. Let chicken stand 10 minutes before slicing. Lightly season onion with salt and pepper, remove from skewers and separate rings.

6. Meanwhile, toast cut sides of bread on grill.

7. To assemble sandwich, lay bread on cutting board cut sides up. Remove reserved marinade from refrigerator, mix well and brush onto both halves of bread. Sprinkle the cilantro onto bottom half. Top with layers of cheese, tomato, chicken and seasoned onions. Top with remaining bread. Press down firmly to allow ingredients to adhere. Wrap sandwich in foil. Place on grill over direct heat. Top with large skillet to flatten. Grill 4 to 6 minutes or until cheese melts.

8. Transfer sandwiches to clean cutting board; cut into six pieces. Serve immediately.

SPICY BBQ CHICKEN PIZZA

MAKES 8 SERVINGS

- 2 cups shredded, cooked chicken (about 1 pound uncooked)
- ¼ cup **FRANK'S® RedHot®** Buffalo Wings Sauce
- 1 pound prepared pizza *or* bread dough (thawed, if frozen)
- 1 cup *Cattlemen's®* Award Winning Classic Barbecue Sauce
- 2 ripe plum tomatoes, diced
- ½ cup finely diced red onion
- ½ cup sliced black olives (2.25-ounce can)
- 2 cups shredded taco blend cheese
- Cilantro or green onions, minced (optional)

1. Toss chicken with **FRANK'S RedHot** Buffalo Wings Sauce; set aside. Divide dough in half. Gently stretch or roll each piece of dough into 13×9-inch rectangle on floured surface. Coat one side with nonstick cooking spray.

2. Cook dough, coated side down, on greased grill over medium-high heat for 5 minutes until browned and crisp on bottom. Using tongs, turn dough over. Spread each pizza crust with barbecue sauce and top with chicken mixture, tomatoes, onion, olives and cheese, dividing evenly.

3. Grill pizzas about 5 minutes longer until bottom is browned, crispy and cheese melts. Garnish with minced cilantro or green onions, if desired.

VARIATION

Top pizza with different shredded cheeses, such as Cheddar or Jack, or wsssith other vegetables, such as whole kernel corn, jalapeño or bell peppers.

TIP

For easier handling, allow pizza dough to rest 30 minutes in an oiled, covered bowl at room temperature.

GINGER-LIME CHICKEN THIGHS ▶

MAKES 2 TO 4 SERVINGS

⅓ cup vegetable oil

3 tablespoons lime juice

3 tablespoons honey

2 teaspoons grated fresh ginger *or* 1 teaspoon ground ginger

¼ to ½ teaspoon red pepper flakes

6 boneless skinless chicken thighs

1. Combine oil, lime juice, honey, ginger and red pepper flakes in small bowl. Place chicken in large resealable food storage bag. Add ½ cup marinade; reserve remaining marinade. Seal bag; turn to coat. Marinate in refrigerator 30 to 60 minutes, turning occasionally.

2. Prepare grill for direct cooking over medium-high heat. Lightly oil grid.

3. Remove chicken from marinade; discard marinade. Grill chicken, 12 minutes or until chicken is cooked through, turning once. Brush with reserved marinade during last 5 minutes of cooking.

FAJITA CHICKEN SALAD

MAKES 4 SERVINGS

1 cup WISH-BONE® Italian Dressing

1 lb. boneless, skinless chicken breast halves

2 large red, green or yellow bell peppers, quartered

1 large sweet onion, quartered

4 fajita-size flour tortillas

6 cups torn romaine lettuce leaves

1 medium lime, cut into wedges (optional)

1. In large, resealable plastic bag, pour ¼ cup Wish-Bone Italian Dressing over chicken; turn to coat. In another large, resealable plastic bag, pour ¼ cup Dressing over red peppers and onion. Close bags and marinate in refrigerator up to 3 hours.

2. Remove chicken and vegetables from marinades, discarding marinades. Grill or broil chicken and vegetables, turning once and brushing frequently with remaining ½ cup Dressing, 12 minutes or until chicken is thoroughly cooked and vegetables are crisp-tender. Lightly grill tortillas, turning once and brushing with additional Dressing, if desired. Tear tortillas into bite-size pieces.

3. To serve, thinly slice chicken and vegetables. Arrange lettuce on serving platter, top with chicken, vegetables, tortillas and lime. Serve, if desired, with additional Dressing.

PESTO-STUFFED GRILLED CHICKEN

MAKES 6 SERVINGS

2 cloves garlic, peeled

½ cup packed fresh basil leaves

2 tablespoons pine nuts or walnuts, toasted*

¼ teaspoon black pepper

5 tablespoons extra virgin olive oil, divided

¼ cup grated Parmesan cheese

1 fresh or thawed frozen roasting chicken or capon (6 to 7 pounds)

2 tablespoons fresh lemon juice

To toast pine nuts, spread in single layer in small heavy skillet. Cook and stir 2 to 3 minutes or until golden brown, stirring frequently.

1. Prepare grill with metal or foil drip pan. Bank briquettes on either side of drip pan for indirect cooking over medium-low heat.

2. For pesto, drop garlic through feed tube of food processor with motor running. Add basil, pine nuts and black pepper; process until basil is minced. With motor running, add 3 tablespoons oil in thin, steady stream until smooth paste forms, scraping down side of bowl once. Add cheese; process until well blended.

3. Remove giblets from chicken cavity; reserve for another use. Loosen skin over breast of chicken by pushing fingers between skin and meat, taking care not to tear skin. Do not loosen skin over wings and drumsticks. Using rubber spatula or small spoon, spread pesto under breast skin; massage skin to evenly spread pesto. Combine remaining 2 tablespoons oil and lemon juice in small bowl; brush over chicken skin. Tuck wings under back; tie legs together with kitchen string.

4. Place chicken, breast side up, on grid directly over drip pan. Grill, covered, 1 hour 10 minutes to 1 hour 30 minutes or until thermometer inserted into thickest part of thigh not touching bone registers 185°F, adding 4 to 9 briquettes to both sides of the fire after 45 minutes to maintain medium-low coals. Transfer chicken to large cutting board; tent with foil. Let stand 15 minutes before carving.

SESAME HOISIN BEER-CAN CHICKEN

MAKES 8 TO 10 SERVINGS

- 1 **can (12 ounces) beer, divided**
- ½ **cup hoisin sauce**
- 2 **tablespoons honey**
- 1 **tablespoon soy sauce**
- 1 **teaspoon chili garlic sauce**
- ½ **teaspoon dark sesame oil**
- 1 **whole chicken (3½ to 4 pounds)**

1. Prepare grill for indirect cooking over medium heat. Lightly oil grid. Combine 2 tablespoons beer, hoisin sauce, honey, soy sauce, chili garlic sauce and oil in small bowl; stir to blend. Gently loosen skin of chicken over breast meat, legs and thighs. Spoon half of hoisin mixture evenly under skin and into cavity. Pour off beer until can is two-thirds full. Hold chicken upright with opening of cavity pointing down. Insert beer can into cavity.

2. Stand chicken upright on can over drip pan. Spread legs slightly to help support chicken. Cover; grill 30 minutes. Brush chicken with remaining hoisin mixture. Cover; grill 45 to 60 minutes or until chicken is cooked through (165°F). Use metal tongs to remove chicken and can to large cutting board; let rest, standing up, 5 minutes. Carefully remove can and discard. Carve chicken and serve.

FAJITA-SEASONED GRILLED CHICKEN ▶

MAKES 2 SERVINGS

2 boneless skinless
  chicken breasts
  (about 4 ounces each)
1 bunch green onions,
  ends trimmed
1 tablespoon olive oil
2 teaspoons fajita
  seasoning mix

1. Prepare grill for direct cooking over medium-high heat. Lightly oil grid.

2. Brush chicken and green onions with oil. Sprinkle both sides of chicken with seasoning mix. Grill chicken and green onions 6 to 8 minutes or until chicken is no longer pink in center.

3. Serve chicken with green onions.

THAI BARBECUED CHICKEN

MAKES 4 SERVINGS

1 cup coarsely chopped
  fresh cilantro
2 jalapeño peppers,
  stemmed and seeded
8 cloves garlic, coarsely
  chopped
2 tablespoons fish sauce
1 tablespoon packed
  brown sugar
1 teaspoon curry powder
  Grated peel of 1 lemon
3 pounds bone-in chicken
  pieces

1. Combine cilantro, jalapeños, garlic, fish sauce, brown sugar, curry powder and lemon peel in food processor or blender; process until coarse paste forms.

2. Work fingers between skin and meat on breast and thigh pieces. Rub about 1 teaspoon seasoning paste under skin on each piece. Rub remaining paste all over chicken pieces. Place chicken in large resealable food storage bag or covered container; refrigerate 3 to 4 hours or overnight.

3. Prepare grill for direct cooking over medium heat. Lightly oil grid.

4. Grill chicken, skin side down, covered, 10 minutes or until well browned. Turn chicken. Grill 20 to 30 minutes or until chicken is cooked through (165°F). (Thighs and legs may require 5 to 10 minutes more cooking time than breasts.) If chicken is browned on both sides but still needs additional cooking, move to edge of grill, away from direct heat, to finish cooking.

BACKYARD BEEF

STEAK PARMESAN

MAKES 2 SERVINGS

- 4 cloves garlic, minced
- 1 tablespoon olive oil
- 1 tablespoon coarse salt
- 1 teaspoon black pepper
- 2 beef T-bone or Porterhouse steaks, cut 1 to 1¼ inch thick (about 2 pounds)
- ¼ cup grated Parmesan cheese

1. Prepare grill for direct cooking over medium-high heat. Lightly oil grid. Combine garlic, oil, salt and pepper in small bowl; press into both sides of steaks. Let stand 15 minutes.

2. Grill steaks, covered, 14 to 19 minutes or until internal temperature reaches 145°F for medium-rare doneness, turning once.

3. Remove steaks to large cutting board; sprinkle with cheese. Tent with foil; let stand 5 minutes. Serve immediately.

TIP

For a smoky flavor, soak 2 cups hickory or oak wood chips in cold water to cover at least 30 minutes. Drain and scatter over hot coals before grilling.

BEEF AND BEER SLIDERS

MAKES 12 SLIDERS

- 6 tablespoons ketchup
- 2 tablespoons mayonnaise
- 2 teaspoons Dijon mustard
- 1½ pounds ground beef
- ½ cup beer
- 1 teaspoon salt
- ½ teaspoon garlic powder
- ½ teaspoon onion powder
- ½ teaspoon ground cumin
- ½ teaspoon dried oregano
- ¼ teaspoon black pepper
- 3 slices sharp Cheddar cheese, cut into 4 pieces
- 12 slider buns or potato dinner rolls
- 12 baby lettuce leaves
- 12 plum tomato slices

1. Combine ketchup, mayonnaise and mustard in small bowl; stir to blend. Set aside.

2. Prepare grill for direct cooking over medium-high heat. Lightly oil grid. Combine beef, beer, salt, garlic powder, onion powder, cumin, oregano and pepper in medium bowl. Shape mixture into 12 (¼-inch-thick) patties.

3. Add half of patties; grill 2 minutes. Turn; top each with 1 piece cheese. Grill 2 minutes or until cheese is melted and patties are cooked through. Remove to large plate; keep warm. Repeat with remaining patties and cheese.

4. Serve sliders on rolls with ketchup mixture, lettuce and tomato.

SZECHUAN GRILLED FLANK STEAK

MAKES 4 TO 6 SERVINGS

1 beef flank steak (1¼ to 1½ pounds)

¼ cup seasoned rice wine vinegar

¼ cup soy sauce

2 tablespoons dark sesame oil

4 cloves garlic, minced

2 teaspoons minced fresh ginger

½ teaspoon red pepper flakes

¼ cup water

½ cup thinly sliced green onions

2 to 3 teaspoons sesame seeds, toasted*

Hot cooked rice (optional)

*To toast sesame seeds, spread seeds in small skillet. Shake skillet over medium-low heat about 3 minutes or until seeds begin to pop and turn golden.

1. Place steak in large resealable food storage bag. Combine vinegar, soy sauce, oil, garlic, ginger and red pepper flakes in small bowl; stir to blend. Pour marinade over steak. Seal bag; turn to coat. Marinate in refrigerator 3 hours, turning once.

2. Prepare grill for direct cooking over medium heat. Remove steak from marinade; reserve marinade in small saucepan. Grill steak, uncovered, 17 to 21 minutes for medium rare to medium or to desired doneness, turning once.

3. Add water to reserved marinade. Bring to a rolling boil over high heat. Boil for 1 minute. Slice steak against the grain into thin slices. Drizzle slices with boiled marinade. Sprinkle with green onions and sesame seeds. Serve with rice, if desired.

MEATY CHILI DOGS

MAKES 12 SERVINGS

- 1 pound ground beef
- ¼ pound Italian sausage, casings removed
- 1 large onion, chopped
- 2 medium stalks celery, diced
- 1 jalapeño pepper, seeded and chopped
- 2 cloves garlic, minced
- 1 tablespoon chili powder
- 2 teaspoons sugar
- 1 can (28 ounces) diced tomatoes
- 1 can (about 15 ounces) pinto beans, rinsed and drained
- 1 can (12 ounces) tomato juice
- 1 cup water
- 12 hot dogs
- 12 hot dogs buns, split and toasted

1. Cook beef, sausage, onion, celery, jalapeño and garlic in 5-quart Dutch oven over medium heat until meat is cooked through and onion is tender, stirring to break up meat. Drain fat.

2. Stir in chili powder and sugar. Add tomatoes, beans, tomato juice and water. Bring to a boil over high heat. Reduce heat to low. Simmer 30 minutes, stirring occasionally.

3. Prepare grill for direct cooking over medium heat. Lightly oil grid. Grill hot dogs 5 to 8 minutes or until heated through, turning often. Place hot dogs in buns. Spoon about ¼ cup chili over each.

BEEF AND PEPPER KABOBS

MAKES 4 SERVINGS

8 ounces sirloin steak (trimmed of fat before weighing)

1 medium clove garlic, minced

2 teaspoons soy sauce

2 teaspoons red wine vinegar

1½ teaspoons Dijon mustard

1 teaspoon olive oil

⅛ teaspoon black pepper

2 small bell peppers, green, red, yellow or orange

4 large green onions

1 tablespoon chicken or vegetable broth

1. Slice steak into 16 (¼-inch) strips; place in glass bowl. Whisk garlic, soy sauce, vinegar, mustard, oil and black pepper in small bowl. Stir half of mixture into beef. Cover; refrigerate 2 to 3 hours, stirring occasionally. Cover remaining marinade and refrigerate.

2. Prepare grill for direct cooking over medium-high heat. Core and seed bell peppers. Cut each into 12 chunks; thread onto four skewers. Grill bell peppers 5 to 7 minutes per side or until well browned and tender. Grill green onions 3 to 5 minutes or until well browned on both sides. Stir broth into reserved marinade. Brush bell peppers and green onions lightly with marinade once during grilling.

3. Thread 4 beef strips onto four skewers. Grill 2 minutes per side, basting once per side with marinade. Remove 1 beef skewer and 1 bell pepper skewer on each of four plates. Coarsely chop green onions and sprinkle over beef and peppers.

CLASSIC CALIFORNIA BURGERS

MAKES 4 SERVINGS

2 tablespoons FRENCH'S® Honey Dijon Mustard

2 tablespoons mayonnaise

2 tablespoons sour cream

1 pound ground beef

2 tablespoons FRENCH'S® Worcestershire Sauce

1⅓ cups FRENCH'S® Cheddar or Original French Fried Onions, divided

½ teaspoon garlic salt

¼ teaspoon ground black pepper

4 hamburger rolls, split and toasted

½ small avocado, sliced

½ cup alfalfa sprouts

1. Combine mustard, mayonnaise and sour cream; set aside.

2. Combine beef, Worcestershire, ⅔ *cup* French Fried Onions and seasonings. Form into 4 patties. Grill over high heat until juices run clear (160°F internal temperature).

3. Place burgers on rolls. Top each with mustard sauce, avocado slices, sprouts and remaining onions, dividing evenly. Cover with top halves of rolls.

BBQ CHEESE BURGERS

Top each burger with 1 slice American cheese, 1 tablespoon barbecue sauce and 2 tablespoons French Fried Onions.

PIZZA BURGERS

Top each burger with pizza sauce, mozzarella cheese and French Fried Onions.

BARBECUE SIRLOIN PACKET

MAKES 4 SERVINGS

1 sheet (18×24 inches) REYNOLDS WRAP® Heavy Duty Foil

DRY RUB

- 2 teaspoons garlic powder
- 2 teaspoons paprika
- 2 teaspoons packed brown sugar
- 2 teaspoons salt
- 2 teaspoons black pepper
- 2 teaspoons cayenne pepper

INGREDIENTS

- 1 pound boneless beef sirloin steak, ½ inch thick, fat trimmed
- ¼ cup chipotle barbecue sauce
- 1 medium yellow onion, thinly sliced
- 1 medium poblano pepper, seeded and cut into thin strips

PREHEAT grill to medium-high indirect heat. For indirect heat, the heat source (coals or gas burner) is on one side of the grill. Place the food on the opposite side with no coals or flame underneath.

COMBINE ingredients for Dry Rub in a small bowl. Cut steak into thin strips. In a large bowl, combine 2 tablespoons of the rub mixture with the beef strips. Stir in barbecue sauce; set aside. Reserve the remaining Dry Rub for other uses.

CENTER onion slices on sheet of REYNOLDS WRAP® Heavy Duty Aluminum Foil. Top with pepper strips. Arrange beef mixture over onion and pepper in an even layer.

BRING up foil sides. Double fold top and ends to seal, making one large foil packet, leaving room for heat circulation inside.

GRILL 20 to 25 minutes in covered grill over indirect heat.

REYNOLDS KITCHENS TIP

To make your own Chipotle Barbecue Sauce, combine ¼ cup barbecue sauce, 1 tablespoon packed dark brown sugar, 1 tablespoon lime juice and 1 to 2 teaspoons chopped chipotle peppers in adobo sauce.

STEAK AND MUSHROOM SKEWERS

MAKES 4 SERVINGS

¼ cup Italian salad dressing

2 tablespoons Worcestershire sauce

¾ pound beef top sirloin steak, cut into 24 (1-inch) cubes

24 medium whole mushrooms (about 12 ounces)

¼ cup mayonnaise

¼ cup sour cream

1 clove garlic, minced

¼ to ½ teaspoon dried rosemary

¼ teaspoon salt

1 medium zucchini, cut into 24 (1-inch) pieces

1 medium green bell pepper, cut into 24 (1-inch) pieces

1. Combine dressing and Worcestershire sauce in small bowl. Reserve 2 tablespoons dressing mixture. Combine beef, mushrooms and remaining dressing mixture in large resealable food storage bag. Seal bag; turn to coat. Marinate in refrigerator 30 to 60 minutes.

2. For sauce, combine mayonnaise, sour cream, garlic, rosemary and salt in small bowl. Cover; refrigerate until ready to use.

3. Prepare grill for direct cooking over medium-high heat. Thread beef, mushrooms, zucchini and bell pepper alternately onto eight 10-inch skewers. Discard remaining marinade.

4. Grill skewers 6 to 8 minutes or to desired doneness, turning occasionally. *Do not overcook.* Before serving, brush with reserved 2 tablespoons dressing mixture. Serve with sauce.

SERVING SUGGESTION

Serve with grilled French bread slices lightly sprayed with nonstick cooking spray and rubbed with fresh garlic, and spring greens with mandarin oranges, onions and raspberry vinaigrette dressing.

PEPPERED BEEF RIB EYE ROAST

MAKES 6 TO 8 SERVINGS

1½ tablespoons black peppercorns

1 boneless beef rib eye roast (about 2½ to 3 pounds), well trimmed

¼ cup Dijon mustard

2 cloves garlic, minced

Sour Cream Sauce (recipe follows)

1. Prepare grill for indirect cooking over medium heat with drip pan in center. Lightly oil grid.

2. Place peppercorns in small resealable food storage bag. Squeeze out excess air; close bag securely. Pound peppercorns using flat side of meat mallet or rolling pin until cracked.

3. Pat roast dry with paper towels. Combine mustard and garlic in small bowl; spread over roast. Sprinkle with pepper.

4. Place roast on grid directly over drip pan. Grill, covered, 1 hour or until internal temperature reaches 135°F for medium rare or 150°F for medium when tested with meat thermometer inserted into the thickest part of roast. (If using charcoal grill, add 4 to 9 briquets to both sides of the fire after 45 minutes to maintain medium heat.)

5. Meanwhile, prepare Sour Cream Sauce. Cover; refrigerate until serving.

6. Remove roast to large cutting board; tent with foil. Let stand 10 to 15 minutes before carving. (Internal temperature will continue to rise 5°F to 10°F during stand time.) Serve with Sour Cream Sauce.

SOUR CREAM SAUCE

MAKES ABOUT 1 CUP

¾ cup sour cream

2 tablespoons prepared horseradish

1 tablespoon balsamic vinegar

½ teaspoon sugar

Combine sour cream, horseradish, vinegar and sugar in small bowl; stir to blend.

BEEF FAJITA SALAD WITH MANGO-SERRANO VINAIGRETTE

MAKES 4 SERVINGS

- 1 beef Top Sirloin Steak boneless, cut 1 inch thick (about 1 pound)
- 3 medium mangos, peeled, cut in half

  Olive oil
- 2 medium poblano peppers
- ½ teaspoon ground black pepper
- 1 large red onion (about 11 ounces), cut into ½-inch-thick slices
- 3 tablespoons fresh lime juice
- 3 tablespoons water
- 1 to 2 serrano peppers
- 3 tablespoons olive oil
- 1 cup radishes, thinly sliced (about 1 bunch)
- 2 tablespoons chopped fresh cilantro

1. Brush mangos lightly with oil. Place mangos and poblano peppers in center of grid over medium, ash-covered coals. Grill peppers, covered, 9 to 10 minutes (gas grill times remain the same) or until skins are completely blackened, turning occasionally. Grill mangos 8 to 14 minutes (gas grill times remain the same) or until very tender, turning occasionally. Place peppers in food-safe plastic bag; close bag. Let stand 15 minutes. Set mangos aside.

2. Press black pepper evenly onto beef steak. Brush onion slices lightly with oil. Place steak in center of grid over medium, ash-covered coals. Arrange onion slices around steak. Grill steak and onion, covered, 11 to 15 minutes (over medium heat on preheated gas grill, 13 to 16 minutes) or until steak is medium rare (145°F) to medium (160°F) doneness and onion is tender, turning occasionally. Keep warm.

3. Meanwhile, prepare Vinaigrette. Cut grilled mangos into ¾-inch pieces. Combine ½ cup mango, lime juice, water and serrano peppers in food processor container. Cover; process until smooth. With motor running, slowly add oil through opening in cover, processing until well blended. Season with salt, as desired. Set aside.

4. Remove and discard skins, stems and seeds from poblano peppers; cut into ¾-inch pieces. Carve steak into slices. Cut onion slices in half. Place beef, remaining mango pieces, onion, peppers and radishes on serving platter. Season with salt, as desired. Drizzle salad with vinaigrette; toss lightly to coat. Sprinkle with cilantro.

COURTESY THE BEEF CHECKOFF

GRILLED WASABI FLANK STEAK

MAKES 2 SERVINGS

6 tablespoons wasabi
   horseradish

2 tablespoons olive oil

1 beef flank steak (1 to
   1½ pounds)

2 large red potatoes, cut
   into ¼-inch-thick slices

¼ cup water

1 teaspoon salt

1. Combine horseradish and oil in small bowl. Spread 2 tablespoons mixture on both sides of steak. Marinate in refrigerator 30 minutes or up to 2 hours.

2. Place potatoes, water and salt in microwavable dish; cover and microwave on HIGH 5 minutes. Drain potatoes. Add 2 tablespoons horseradish mixture; toss to coat.

3. Prepare grill for direct cooking over medium heat. Lightly oil grid.

4. Grill steak, covered, 8 minutes. Turn steak. Place potatoes on grid. Brush potatoes; then steak with remaining horseradish mixture. Grill 8 to 10 minutes or until steak is medium rare (145°F) and potatoes are slightly browned. Season with salt.

TIJUANA T-BONES

MAKES 4 SERVINGS

1½ cups Pace® Picante
Sauce

2½ teaspoons ground cumin

4 beef T-bone steaks
(about 8 ounces
each), ½-inch thick

2 tablespoons fresh lime
juice

¼ cup chopped fresh
cilantro leaves

1 can (about 15 ounces)
black beans, rinsed
and drained

1 large avocado, peeled,
pitted and chopped
(about 1½ cups)

1. Stir **1 cup** of the picante sauce and **2 teaspoons** of
the cumin in a 3-quart shallow, nonmetallic dish or
gallon-size resealable plastic bag. Add the steaks and
turn them over to coat with the marinade. Cover the dish
or seal the plastic bag and refrigerate for 1 hour, turning
the steaks over a few times while they're marinating.

2. Stir the remaining picante sauce and cumin, lime juice,
cilantro, beans and avocado in a 2-quart bowl and set it
aside.

3. Lightly oil the grill rack and heat the grill to medium.
Remove the steaks from the marinade. Discard any
remaining marinade.

4. Grill the steaks for 12 minutes for medium-rare* or
to desired doneness, turning the steak over halfway
through grilling. Serve the steaks with the salsa mixture.

*The internal temperature of the meat should reach 145°F.

CARNE ASADA

MAKES 4 SERVINGS

2 boneless beef top loin (strip) steaks, cut 1 inch thick (about 10 ounces *each*)

2 teaspoons ground cumin

2 large cloves garlic, minced

2 lime wedges

½ to 1 cup prepared guacamole

Additional lime wedges (optional)

1. Combine cumin and garlic; press evenly onto beef steaks.

2. Place steaks on grid over medium, ash-covered coals. Grill, uncovered, 15 to 18 minutes (over medium heat on preheated gas grill, covered, 11 to 15 minutes) for medium rare (145°F) to medium (160°F) doneness, turning occasionally.

3. Squeeze juice from 1 lime wedge over each steak. Carve steaks into thin slices. Serve with guacamole; garnish with lime wedges, if desired.

COURTESY THE BEEF CHECKOFF

GRILLED REUBEN BURGERS

MAKES 6 SERVINGS

1½ pounds ground beef

½ cup water

½ cup shredded Swiss
    cheese (about
    2 ounces)

1 envelope LIPTON®
    RECIPE SECRETS®
    Onion Soup Mix*

1 tablespoon crisp-
    cooked crumbled
    bacon or bacon bits

½ teaspoon caraway seeds
    (optional)

*Also terrific with LIPTON®
RECIPE SECRETS® Onion
Mushroom Soup Mix.*

1. In large bowl, combine all ingredients; shape into
6 patties.

2. Grill or broil until done. Top, if desired, with heated
sauerkraut and additional bacon.

ASIAN GRILLED STEAK

MAKES 4 SERVINGS

¾ cup WISH-BONE® Italian Dressing*

3 Tbsp. soy sauce

3 Tbsp. firmly packed brown sugar

½ tsp. ground ginger (optional)

1 (1- to 1½-lb.) flank, top round or sirloin steak

Also terrific with WISH-BONE® Robusto Italian, Light Italian or Red Wine Vinaigrette Dressing.

1. Combine all ingredients except steak in small bowl. Pour ½ cup marinade over steak in large, shallow nonaluminum baking dish or resealable plastic bag. Cover, or close bag, and marinate in refrigerator, turning occasionally, 30 minutes or up to 24 hours. Refrigerate remaining marinade.

2. Remove steak from marinade, discarding marinade. Grill or broil steak, turning once and brushing frequently with reserved marinade, until steak is desired doneness. Let stand 10 minutes; thinly slice and serve.

BEER GRILLED STEAKS ▶

MAKES 4 SERVINGS

1 cup light-colored beer, such as lager

¼ cup soy sauce

2 tablespoons molasses

2 cloves garlic, minced

½ teaspoon salt

¼ teaspoon black pepper

4 beef rib eye steaks, 1 inch thick (4 to 6 ounces each)

1. Whisk beer, soy sauce, molasses, garlic, salt and pepper in small bowl. Place steaks in large resealable food storage bag; add beer mixture. Marinate in refrigerator at least 2 hours.

2. Prepare grill for direct cooking over high heat. Grill steaks, covered, 8 to 10 minutes per side to at least 145°F or to desired degree of doneness.

BEST EVER CHILI

MAKES 8 SERVINGS

1½ pounds ground beef

1 cup chopped onion

1 can (about 15 ounces) light kidney beans, drained with 1 cup liquid reserved

1 can (about 15 ounces) dark kidney beans, drained

1½ pounds plum tomatoes, diced

1 can (about 15 ounces) tomato paste

3 slices thick-cut bacon, cooked, chopped and divided

3 to 6 tablespoons chili powder

Chopped fresh cilantro (optional)

1. Brown beef and onion in large cast-iron skillet over medium-high heat 6 to 8 minutes, stirring to break up meat. Drain fat.

2. Prepare grill for direct cooking over medium heat.

3. Add beans, bean liquid, tomatoes, tomato paste, half of bacon and chili powder; mix well. Place skillet on grill. Cover; grill 20 minutes or until beans are heated through. Top with remaining half of bacon and cilantro, if desired.

FLAMIN' SEAFOOD

BOURBON-MARINATED SALMON

MAKES 4 SERVINGS

¼ cup packed brown sugar

¼ cup bourbon

¼ cup soy sauce

2 tablespoons lime juice

1 tablespoon grated fresh ginger

1 tablespoon minced garlic

¼ teaspoon black pepper

4 salmon fillets (7 to 8 ounces each)

2 tablespoons minced green onion

1. Combine brown sugar, bourbon, soy sauce, lime juice, ginger, garlic and pepper in medium bowl; stir to blend. Reserve ¼ cup mixture for serving; set aside.

2. Place salmon in large resealable food storage bag. Pour remaining marinade over salmon; seal bag and turn to coat. Marinate in refrigerator 2 to 4 hours, turning occasionally.

3. Prepare grill for direct cooking over medium heat. Lightly oil grid. Remove salmon from marinade; discard marinade.

4. Grill salmon, covered, 10 minutes or until fish begins to flake when tested with fork. Brush with reserved ¼ cup marinade mixture; sprinkle with green onion.

PEACH BOURBON BBQ BACON-WRAPPED SCALLOPS

MAKES 4 SERVINGS

⅔ cup barbecue sauce

¼ cup peach preserves

1 tablespoon bourbon

16 to 20 slices bacon (do not use thick-cut)

16 to 20 medium sea scallops (about 1¼ pounds)

1 tablespoon olive oil

Salt and black pepper

Hot cooked herbed rice (optional)

1. Combine barbecue sauce, preserves and bourbon in small saucepan; bring to a simmer over medium heat. Reduce heat to low. Simmer 10 minutes.

2. Arrange half of bacon on paper towel-lined microwavable plate; cover with paper towel. Microwave on HIGH 4 minutes or until bacon is partially cooked (not crisp). Repeat with remaining half of bacon.

3. Working with one scallop at a time, wrap one slice of bacon around each scallop; thread onto metal skewers (preferably double pronged skewers).* Thread 4 or 5 bacon-wrapped scallops onto each skewer depending on size of scallops and length of skewers.

4. Prepare grill for direct cooking over medium heat. Lightly oil grid.

5. Brush scallops lightly with oil; sprinkle with salt and pepper. Grill, covered, 4 minutes per side or until bacon is crisp and scallops are opaque, brushing both sides of scallops with sauce during last minute of cooking. Serve scallops with remaining sauce over rice, if desired.

If metal skewers are unavailable, use wooden skewers. Soak in water 30 minutes before grilling to prevent burning.

GRILLED SEA BASS WITH RIPE OLIVE 'N' CAPER SALSA

MAKES 8 SERVINGS

- 1 cup sliced California Ripe Olives
- ½ cup seeded, diced Roma tomatoes
- ½ cup chopped oil-packed sun-dried tomatoes
- ¼ cup minced red onion
- ¼ cup chopped fresh basil
- 3 tablespoons capers
- 2 tablespoons chopped fresh parsley
- 2 tablespoons balsamic-style vinaigrette dressing
- 1 teaspoon minced garlic
- 8 (6-ounce) sea bass or other white fish fillets

  Olive oil

Preheat grill or broiler. Combine all ingredients except sea bass and olive oil in large bowl. Mix well. Adjust seasoning with salt and pepper. Cover and chill. Brush both sides of fillets with olive oil and season with salt and pepper. Grill or broil until fish is firm to the touch, about 5 minutes on each side. Serve each fillet with about ¼ cup of Ripe Olive 'n' Caper Salsa.

CALIFORNIA OLIVE COMMITTEE

BEER AND ORANGE MARINATED TUNA STEAKS

MAKES 4 SERVINGS

NECTARINE SALSA

- 2 large nectarines, pitted and cut into ½-inch dice
- 3 tablespoons finely chopped red onion
- ½ jalapeño pepper, finely chopped
- 2 tablespoons fresh chopped cilantro
- 1 tablespoon lime juice
- ¼ teaspoon salt

TUNA

- ½ cup beer
- ⅓ cup chopped green onions
- ¼ cup orange juice
- ¼ cup soy sauce
- 2 tablespoons lemon juice
- 2 tablespoons grated fresh ginger
- 2 cloves garlic, minced
- 2 tablespoons sugar
- 4 (6 to 8 ounces) tuna steaks, about ¾ inch thick

1. For salsa, combine nectarines, onion, jalapeño, cilantro, lime juice and salt in medium bowl; toss to blend.

2. For tuna, combine beer, green onions, orange juice, soy sauce, lemon juice, ginger, garlic and sugar in large bowl; mix well. Add tuna, turning to coat. Refrigerate 30 minutes, turning occasionally.

3. Prepare grill for direct cooking over medium-high heat. Lightly oil grid.

4. Remove tuna from marinade; discard marinade. Grill tuna 3 minutes per side or until marked and pink in center. Remove to serving plates. Serve with salsa.

GRILLED HALIBUT WITH CHERRY TOMATO RELISH

MAKES 4 SERVINGS

3 tablespoons fresh lemon juice, divided

2 teaspoons grated lemon peel, divided

2 cloves garlic, minced

2 teaspoons olive oil, divided

¼ teaspoon salt, divided

¼ teaspoon black pepper, divided

4 halibut fillets (about 6 ounces each)

2 cups cherry tomatoes, quartered

2 tablespoons chopped fresh parsley

1. Combine 2 tablespoons lemon juice, 1 teaspoon lemon peel, garlic, 1 teaspoon oil, ⅛ teaspoon salt and ⅛ teaspoon pepper in large resealable food storage bag. Add halibut; seal bag. Refrigerate 1 hour.

2. Combine tomatoes, parsley, remaining 1 tablespoon lemon juice, 1 teaspoon lemon peel, 1 teaspoon oil, ⅛ teaspoon salt and ⅛ teaspoon pepper in medium bowl; set aside.

3. Prepare grill for direct cooking over medium heat. Lightly oil grid.

4. Remove halibut from marinade; discard marinade. Grill halibut, covered, 3 to 5 minutes per side or until fish begins to flake when tested with fork. Serve with relish.

MOJITO SHRIMP COCKTAIL

MAKES 6 TO 8 SERVINGS

1 pound frozen medium raw shrimp, deveined but not peeled (with tails on)

1 cup plus 2 tablespoons prepared mojito cocktail mix, divided

2 tablespoons olive oil

1 jar shrimp cocktail sauce

Lime wedges (optional)

1. Place shrimp in large shallow glass dish. Pour 1 cup mojito mix over shrimp to cover. (Separate shrimp as much as possible to aid thawing.) Marinate in refrigerator 10 to 24 hours or until thawed, stirring shrimp once or twice.

2. Prepare grill for direct cooking over medium-high heat. Lightly oil grid.

3. Drain shrimp; discard marinade. *Do not peel.* Pat dry and place in large bowl with oil; toss to coat. Grill shrimp, 10 to 15 minutes or until shrimp are pink and opaque, turning once. Refrigerate until ready to serve.

4. Pour cocktail sauce into serving bowl; add remaining 1 to 2 tablespoons mojito mix and stir to combine. Peel shrimp before serving or provide bowl for shells. Serve with lime wedges, if desired.

VARIATION

Add fresh chopped mint to cocktail sauce instead of, or in addition to, mojito mix.

TROUT STUFFED WITH FRESH MINT AND ORANGE

MAKES 6 SERVINGS

2 pan-dressed* trout (1 to 1¼ pounds each)

½ teaspoon coarse salt

1 orange, sliced

1 cup fresh mint leaves

1 sweet onion, sliced

A pan-dressed trout has been gutted and scaled with head and tail removed.

1. Prepare grill for direct cooking over medium heat. Spray two large sheets of foil with nonstick cooking spray.

2. Rinse trout under cold running water; pat dry with paper towels. Sprinkle cavities of trout with salt; fill each with orange slices and mint. Cover each fish with onion slices. Place 1 fish on each prepared sheet of foil; seal using drugstore wrap technique.**

3. Grill trout, covered, 20 to 25 minutes or until trout flakes easily when tested with fork, turning once. Carefully open foil packets, avoiding hot steam. Remove and discard orange-mint stuffing and trout skin before serving.

**Place the fish in the center of an oblong piece of heavy-duty foil, leaving at least a two-inch border around the food. Bring the two long sides together above the food; fold down in a series of locked folds, allowing for heat circulation and expansion. Fold the short ends up and over again. Press folds firmly to seal the foil packet.*

GRILLED TILAPIA WITH ZESTY MUSTARD SAUCE

MAKES 4 SERVINGS

- 2 tablespoons olive oil
- 2 tablespoons butter
- 1 teaspoon Dijon mustard
- ½ teaspoon grated lemon peel
- ½ teaspoon Worcestershire sauce
- ¼ teaspoon black pepper
- 4 mild thin fish fillets, such as tilapia (about 4 ounces each)
- 1½ teaspoons paprika
- ¼ teaspoon salt
- ½ medium lemon, quartered
- 2 tablespoons minced fresh parsley (optional)

1. Prepare grill for direct cooking over high heat. Lightly oil grill basket.

2. Combine butter, mustard, lemon peel, Worcestershire sauce and pepper in small bowl; stir until well blended. Set aside.

3. Rinse fish and pat dry with paper towels. Sprinkle both sides of fish with paprika and salt. Place fish in prepared basket. Grill fish, covered, 6 minutes or until fish flakes easily when tested with fork, turning halfway through cooking time. Remove to medium serving platter.

4. Squeeze one lemon wedge over each fillet. Spread butter mixture evenly over fish; garnish with parsley.

CEDAR PLANK SALMON WITH GRILLED CITRUS MANGO

MAKES 4 SERVINGS

4 salmon fillets (6 ounces each), skin intact

2 teaspoons sugar, divided

1 teaspoon chili powder

½ teaspoon black pepper

¼ teaspoon salt

¼ teaspoon ground allspice

2 tablespoons orange juice

1 tablespoon lemon juice

1 tablespoon lime juice

2 teaspoons minced fresh ginger

¼ cup chopped fresh mint

⅛ teaspoon red pepper flakes

2 medium mangoes, peeled and cut into 1-inch pieces

1 cedar plank (about 15×7 inches, ½ inch thick), soaked*

Soak in water 5 hours or overnight.

1. Prepare grill for direct cooking over medium-high heat.

2. Rinse and pat dry salmon fillets. Combine 1 teaspoon sugar, chili powder, black pepper, salt and allspice in small bowl; stir to blend. Rub evenly over flesh side of fillets. Set aside.

3. Combine remaining 1 teaspoon sugar; orange, lemon and lime juices; ginger; mint and red pepper flakes in medium bowl; stir to blend.

4. Thread mango pieces onto skewers or spread out in grill basket.

5. If using charcoal grill, wait until coals are covered with gray ash to start grilling salmon. If using gas grill, turn heat down to medium. Keep clean spray bottle filled with water nearby in case plank** begins to burn. If it flares up, spray lightly with water.

6. Place soaked plank on grid. Heat, covered, until plank smokes and crackles. Place salmon, skin side down, on plank and arrange mango skewers alongside plank. Grill, covered, 6 to 8 minutes, turning skewers frequently, until mango pieces are slightly charred. Remove mango from the grill; set aside. Cover; grill salmon 9 to 12 minutes or until the flesh begins to flake when tested with fork.

7. Remove plank from grill and transfer salmon to serving platter. Slide mango pieces off skewers and add to mint mixture, tossing gently to coat. Serve immediately alongside salmon.

*__**Cedar planks can be purchased at gourmet kitchen stores or hardware stores. Be sure to buy untreated wood at least ½-inch thick. Use each plank for grilling food only once. Used planks may be broken up into wood chips and used to smoke foods.__*

SURF & TURF KABOBS

MAKES 4 SERVINGS

1 pound beef tenderloin, cut into 1¼-inch pieces

12 raw jumbo shrimp, peeled and deveined (with tails on)

1 medium onion, cut into 12 wedges

1 red or yellow bell pepper, cut into 1-inch pieces

⅓ cup butter, melted

3 tablespoons lemon juice

3 cloves garlic, minced

2 teaspoons paprika or smoked paprika

½ teaspoon salt

¼ teaspoon black pepper or ground red pepper

Lemon wedges

1. Prepare grill for direct cooking over medium heat. Lightly oil grid. Alternately thread beef, shrimp, onion and bell pepper onto four 12-inch metal skewers. (Skewer shrimp through ends to form "C" shape for even cooking.)

2. Combine butter, lemon juice, garlic, paprika, salt and black pepper in small bowl; brush half of mixture over kabobs.

3. Grill kabobs 5 minutes; turn and brush with remaining butter mixture. Grill 5 to 6 minutes or until shrimp are pink and opaque (beef will be medium-rare to medium doneness). Serve with lemon wedges.

TIP

Be sure to purchase jumbo shrimp for this recipe. The shrimp and steak should be approximately the same size so they will cook evenly.

BLACKENED CATFISH WITH CREOLE VEGETABLES

MAKES 4 SERVINGS

⅔ cup **Cattlemen's**®
    Authentic Smoke
    House Barbecue
    Sauce or **Cattlemen's**®
    Award Winning Classic
    Barbecue Sauce

⅓ cup FRANK'S® REDHOT®
    Original Cayenne
    Pepper Sauce

2 tablespoons Southwest
    chile seasoning
    blend or Cajun blend
    seasoning

1 tablespoon olive oil

4 skinless catfish or
    sea bass fillets
    (1½ pounds)

Salt and pepper to taste

Creole Vegetables
    (recipe follows)

1. Combine barbecue sauce, *Original Cayenne Pepper Sauce*, seasoning blend and oil. Reserve ½ cup mixture for Creole Vegetables.

2. Season fish with salt and pepper to taste. Baste fish with remaining barbecue mixture.

3. Cook fish on a well-greased grill over medium direct heat 5 minutes per side until fish is opaque in center, turning once. Serve with Creole Vegetables.

CREOLE VEGETABLES

MAKES 4 SERVINGS

1 red, green or orange
    bell pepper, cut into
    quarters

1 large green zucchini or
    summer squash, cut
    in half crosswise, then
    lengthwise into thick
    slices

1 large white onion, sliced
    ½ inch thick

Vegetable cooking spray

Arrange vegetables on skewers. Coat vegetables with cooking spray. Grill vegetables over medium direct heat until lightly charred and tender, basting often with reserved ½ cup barbecue sauce mixture.

FISH TACOS WITH YOGURT SAUCE

MAKES 6 SERVINGS

SAUCE

- ½ cup plain yogurt
- ¼ cup chopped fresh cilantro
- 3 tablespoons sour cream
- Juice of 1 lime
- 1 tablespoon mayonnaise
- ½ teaspoon ground cumin
- ¼ teaspoon ground red pepper
- Salt and black pepper

TACOS

- Juice of ½ lime
- 2 tablespoons canola oil
- 1½ pounds swordfish, halibut or tilapia fillets
- Salt and black pepper
- 12 corn or flour tortillas
- 3 cups shredded cabbage or prepared coleslaw mixture
- 2 medium tomatoes, chopped

1. For sauce, mix yogurt, cilantro, sour cream, lime juice, mayonnaise, cumin and red pepper in small bowl. Season with salt and black pepper.

2. Prepare grill for direct cooking over high heat. Lightly oil grid.

3. For tacos, combine juice of ½ lime and oil in small bowl. Brush or spoon lime and oil mixture over fish fillets about 5 minutes before cooking. Season with salt and black pepper. (Do not marinate fish longer than 5 minutes, or acid in lime will begin to "cook" fish.)

4. Grill fish, covered, 10 minutes, turning once. Flake fish or break into large pieces.

5. Place tortillas on grill over medium heat. Grill 10 seconds on each side or until beginning to bubble and brown lightly. Fill tortillas with fish. Top with sauce, cabbage and tomatoes.

COD & LEMON RICE PILAF PACKETS

MAKES 4 SERVINGS

- 4 sheets (12×18 inches each) REYNOLDS WRAP® Non-Stick Foil
- 2 packages (4.2 ounces each) rice and sauce pilaf
- 4 cod or flounder fillets (4 to 6 ounces each)
- 1½ teaspoons lemon pepper seasoning
  - Grated peel and juice of 1 lemon
- ½ medium red bell pepper, chopped
- ¼ cup sliced almonds, toasted

PREHEAT grill to medium-high or oven to 450°F. Prepare pilaf mix following package directions; set aside.

CENTER one fish fillet on each sheet of REYNOLDS WRAP® Non-Stick Foil. Sprinkle with lemon pepper seasoning. Add lemon peel and juice to cooked pilaf; spoon pilaf beside fish. Spoon red pepper over fish and rice.

BRING up foil sides. Double fold top and ends to seal packet, leaving room for heat circulation inside. Repeat to make four packets.

GRILL 10 to 12 minutes in covered grill **OR BAKE** 12 to 14 minutes on a cookie sheet in oven. Sprinkle with almonds before serving.

REYNOLDS KITCHENS TIP

Toast almonds in skillet over medium-high heat, stirring constantly until browned.

BARBECUED SHRIMP OVER TROPICAL RICE

MAKES 4 SERVINGS

20 frozen large raw shrimp, peeled and deveined (26 to 30 per pound)

½ cup uncooked brown rice

2 tablespoons olive oil

½ cup barbecue sauce

2 teaspoons fresh grated ginger

1 cup chopped fresh mango* (about 1 medium mango)

2 tablespoons finely chopped red onion

1 tablespoon chopped fresh cilantro

1 tablespoon finely chopped and seeded jalapeño pepper

2 teaspoons lime juice

To chop a mango, first cut off all four sides around the pit. Then slide a knife between the skin and meat of the mango. Remove skin and cut into chunks then chop into smaller pieces.

1. Thaw shrimp according to package directions. Cook rice according to package directions, omitting salt; set aside.

2. Prepare grill for direct cooking over medium heat. Lightly oil grid. Thread shrimp onto four metal skewers, leaving ⅛-inch space between shrimp. Combine barbecue sauce and ginger in small bowl; stir to blend.

3. Grill shrimp, uncovered, 6 to 7 minutes or until shrimp are opaque, turning once and brushing frequently with sauce mixture.

4. Stir mango, onion, cilantro, jalapeño and lime juice into hot rice. Spoon onto serving plates. Serve shrimp on top of rice mixture.

GRILLED SCALLOPS AND VEGETABLES WITH CILANTRO SAUCE

MAKES 4 SERVINGS

1 teaspoon hot chili oil

1 teaspoon dark sesame oil

1 green onion, chopped

1 tablespoon finely chopped fresh ginger

1 cup chicken broth

1 cup chopped fresh cilantro

1 pound raw or thawed frozen sea scallops

2 medium zucchini, cut into ½-inch slices

2 medium yellow squash, cut into ½-inch slices

1 medium yellow onion, cut into wedges

8 large mushrooms

1. Prepare grill for direct cooking. Lightly oil grid.

2. Heat chili oil and sesame oil in small saucepan over medium-low heat. Add green onion; cook and stir 15 seconds or just until fragrant. Add ginger; cook and stir 1 minute. Stir in broth; bring to a boil. Cook until liquid is reduced by half; cool slightly. Pour into blender or food processor; add cilantro and blend until smooth. (Or add cilantro to saucepan and use hand-held immersion blender to blend mixture until smooth.)

3. Thread scallops and vegetables onto four 12-inch skewers.*

4. Grill over medium-high heat 8 minutes per side or until scallops turn opaque. Serve hot with cilantro sauce.

If using wooden skewers, soak in water 25 to 30 minutes before using to prevent skewers from burning.

PLEASING PORK

TERIYAKI PORK KABOBS

MAKES 4 SERVINGS

- 2 tablespoons cornstarch
- 1¾ cups Swanson® Beef Stock
- 2 tablespoons soy sauce
- 1 tablespoon packed brown sugar
- ½ teaspoon garlic powder* **or** 2 cloves garlic, minced
- ¼ teaspoon ground ginger
- 1 pound boneless pork loin, cut into 1-inch cubes
- 12 medium mushrooms
- 1 large red onion, cut into 12 wedges
- 4 cherry tomatoes
- 4 cups hot cooked regular long-grain white rice

1. Stir the cornstarch, stock, soy sauce, brown sugar, garlic powder and ginger in a 2-quart saucepan until the mixture is smooth. Cook and stir over medium heat until the mixture boils and thickens. Remove the saucepan from the heat.

2. Thread alternately the pork, mushrooms and onion on 4 skewers.

3. Lightly oil the grill rack and heat the grill to medium. Grill the kabobs for 20 minutes or until the pork is cooked through, turning and brushing often with the stock mixture. Thread 1 tomato on each skewer.

4. Heat the remaining stock mixture to a boil over medium-high heat. Serve the stock mixture with the kabobs and rice.

MARINATED ITALIAN SAUSAGE AND PEPPERS

MAKES 4 SERVINGS

½ cup olive oil

¼ cup red wine vinegar

2 tablespoons chopped fresh parsley

1 tablespoon dried oregano

2 cloves garlic, crushed

1 teaspoon salt

1 teaspoon black pepper

4 links hot or sweet Italian sausage

1 large onion, cut into rings

1 large bell pepper, cut into quarters

Horseradish-Mustard Spread (recipe follows)

1. Combine oil, vinegar, parsley, oregano, garlic, salt and black pepper in small bowl. Place sausage, onion and bell pepper in large resealable food storage bag; pour oil mixture over sausage and vegetables. Seal bag; turn to coat. Marinate in refrigerator 1 to 2 hours.

2. Prepare Horseradish-Mustard Spread; set aside. Prepare grill for direct cooking over medium heat. Lightly oil grid.

3. Remove sausage, onion and bell pepper from marinade; reserve marinade. Grill sausage, covered, 5 minutes. Turn sausage and place onion and bell pepper on grid; brush with reserved marinade. Discard remaining marinade. Grill, covered, 5 minutes or until sausage is cooked through and vegetables are crisp-tender. Serve sausage and vegetables with Horseradish-Mustard Spread.

HORSERADISH-MUSTARD SPREAD

MAKES ABOUT ¼ CUP

3 tablespoons mayonnaise

1 tablespoon chopped fresh parsley

1 tablespoon prepared horseradish

1 tablespoon Dijon mustard

2 teaspoons garlic powder

1 teaspoon black pepper

Combine mayonnaise, parsley, horseradish, mustard, garlic powder and pepper in small bowl; stir to blend.

CUBANO BURGERS

MAKES 4 SERVINGS

- 1½ pounds ground pork
- ¼ cup minced green onions
- 3 tablespoons yellow mustard, divided
- 1 tablespoon minced garlic
- 2 teaspoons paprika
- ½ teaspoon black pepper
- ¼ teaspoon salt
- 8 slices Swiss cheese
- 4 Kaiser rolls or bolillos, split and toasted
- 8 slices sandwich-style dill pickles
- ¼ pound thinly sliced ham

1. Prepare grill for direct cooking over medium heat. Lightly oil grid.

2. Combine pork, green onions, 1 tablespoon mustard, garlic, paprika, pepper and salt in large bowl; mix lightly but thoroughly. Shape into four patties about ¾ inch thick, shaping to fit rolls.

3. Grill patties, covered, 8 to 10 minutes (or uncovered, 13 to 15 minutes) or until cooked through (160°F), turning occasionally. Top each burger with 2 slices Swiss cheese during last 2 minutes of grilling.

4. Spread remaining 2 tablespoons mustard over cut sides of rolls. Place pickles on bottom half of each roll. Top each with burger and ham. Cover with top halves of rolls. Press down firmly.

NOTE

Traditional Cuban sandwiches are made with sliced roast pork and do not include mayonnaise, tomatoes, onions, bell peppers or lettuce. Thinly sliced plantain chips usually accompany the sandwiches.

PORK AND PLUM KABOBS

MAKES 4 SERVINGS

¾ **pound boneless pork loin chops (1 inch thick), trimmed and cut into 1-inch pieces**

1½ **teaspoons ground cumin**

½ **teaspoon ground cinnamon**

¼ **teaspoon salt**

¼ **teaspoon garlic powder**

¼ **teaspoon ground red pepper**

¼ **cup sliced green onions**

¼ **cup raspberry fruit spread**

1 **tablespoon orange juice**

3 **plums or nectarines, pitted and cut into wedges**

1. Place pork in large resealable food storage bag. Combine cumin, cinnamon, salt, garlic powder and red pepper in small bowl; pour over pork. Seal bag; shake to coat meat with spices.

2. Combine green onions, fruit spread and orange juice in small bowl; set aside.

3. Prepare grill for direct cooking over medium heat. Lightly oil grid. Alternately thread pork and plum wedges onto eight skewers.* Grill kabobs, covered, 12 to 14 minutes or until meat is cooked through, turning once. Brush frequently with raspberry mixture during last 5 minutes of grilling.

If using wood skewers, soak in warm water 30 minutes to prevent burning.

SERVING SUGGESTION

A crisp, cool salad makes a great accompaniment to these sweet grilled kabobs.

PORK FAJITAS WITH MANGO AND SALSA VERDE

MAKES 4 SERVINGS

- 2 **cloves garlic, crushed**
- 2 **teaspoons chili powder**
- ½ **teaspoon ground cumin**
- ½ **teaspoon ground coriander**
- 12 **ounces pork tenderloin, trimmed of fat**
- 1 **medium red onion, cut into ½-inch rings**
- 1 **mango, peeled and cut into ½-inch pieces**
- 8 **(6-inch) flour tortillas, warmed**
- ½ **cup salsa verde**

1. Prepare grill for direct cooking over medium-high heat. Lightly oil grid.

2. Combine garlic, chili powder, cumin and coriander in small bowl; stir to blend. Rub evenly onto pork.

3. Grill pork 12 to 16 minutes or until thermometer registers 155°F for medium doneness, turning occasionally. During last 8 minutes of grilling, grill onion until tender, turning occasionally.

4. Remove onion to small bowl. Remove pork to large cutting board; tent loosely with foil. Let stand 5 to 10 minutes before slicing into ½-inch strips.

5. Arrange pork, onion and mango on tortillas. Spoon evenly with salsa verde. Fold bottom 3 inches of each tortilla up over filling; roll up to enclose filling.

THAI-STYLE PORK CHOPS WITH CUCUMBER SAUCE

MAKES 4 SERVINGS

- 3 tablespoons Thai peanut sauce, divided
- ¼ teaspoon red pepper flakes
- 4 bone-in pork chops (5 ounces each)
- 1 container (6 ounces) plain yogurt
- ¼ cup diced unpeeled cucumber
- 2 tablespoons chopped red onion
- 2 tablespoons finely chopped fresh mint or cilantro
- 1 teaspoon sugar

1. Combine 2 tablespoons peanut sauce and red pepper flakes in small bowl; brush mixture evenly over both sides of pork chops. Let stand while preparing cucumber sauce, or refrigerate up to 4 hours.

2. Prepare grill for direct cooking over medium heat. Lightly oil grid. Combine yogurt, cucumber, onion, mint and sugar in medium bowl; mix well.

3. Grill pork chops, covered, 4 minutes. Turn. Grill 3 minutes or until barely pink in center. Just before removing from heat, baste with remaining 1 tablespoon peanut sauce. Serve chops with cucumber sauce.

SERVING SUGGESTION

Serve with hot cooked rice, steamed carrots and broccoli and/or sliced ripe mango or papaya.

MIXED GRILL KABOBS
MAKES 6 TO 8 SERVINGS

1 pound boneless beef sirloin, cut into 1-inch cubes

2 large red, orange or yellow bell peppers, cut into chunks

12 strips bacon, blanched*

12 ounces smoked sausage or kielbasa, cut into ½-inch slices

1 cup peeled red pearl onions or red onion chunks

1 pound pork tenderloin, cut lengthwise in half, then into ¼-inch wide long strips

1 cup pineapple wedges

1½ cups *Cattlemen's*® Award Winning Classic Barbecue Sauce

*To blanch bacon, place bacon strips into boiling water for 1 minute. Drain thoroughly.

1. Arrange beef cubes and 1 bell pepper on metal skewers, weaving bacon strips around all. Place sausage, 1 pepper and onions on separate skewers. Ribbon strips of pork on additional skewers with pineapple wedges.

2. Baste the different kabobs with some of the barbecue sauce. Cook on a well-greased grill over medium-high direct heat, basting often with remaining barbecue sauce.

3. Serve a trio of kabobs to each person with additional sauce.

TIP

To easily cut pork, freeze about 30 minutes until very firm.

NOTE

You may substitute *Cattlemen's*® Authentic Smoke House or Golden Honey Barbecue Sauce.

PORK TENDERLOIN CUBANO WITH MANGO MOJO

MAKES 6 SERVINGS

1 whole pork tenderloin, butterflied (about 1½ pounds)

1 cup Pace® Picante Sauce

7½ ounces cooked chorizo sausage **or** pepperoni, chopped (about 2 cups)

½ cup Pepperidge Farm® Onion and Garlic Croutons, crushed

1 cup orange juice

3 tablespoons chopped fresh cilantro leaves

2 tablespoons packed brown sugar

1 ripe mango, peeled, seeded and chopped (about 1½ cups)

1. Place the pork between **2** sheets of plastic wrap. Working from the center, pound the pork flat into a 14×6-inch rectangle. Remove the plastic wrap.

2. Stir ½ **cup** picante sauce, the chorizo and croutons in a medium bowl. Spread the chorizo mixture lengthwise down the center of the pork. Fold the sides over the filling. Tie the pork crosswise at 2-inch intervals with kitchen twine.

3. Place the remaining picante sauce, orange juice, cilantro, brown sugar and mango into a blender. Cover and blend until the mixture is smooth. Pour the mango mixture into a 10-inch skillet. Heat over medium-high heat to a boil. Reduce the heat to medium-low. Cook and stir for 20 minutes or until the sauce is thickened.

4. Lightly oil the grill rack and heat the grill to medium. Grill the pork for 20 minutes or until it's cooked through, turning the pork over once halfway through grilling. Remove the pork from the grill and let stand for 10 minutes. Thinly slice the pork and serve with the mango sauce.

KITCHEN TIP

When choosing a mango, look for firmness. A ripe mango is slightly soft to the touch. It will continue to ripen at room temperature, so if you don't use it immediately you can store it in the refrigerator for about 5 days.

PORK TENDERLOIN SLIDERS

MAKES 12 SANDWICHES

2 teaspoons chili powder

¾ teaspoon ground cumin

½ teaspoon salt

½ teaspoon black pepper

2 tablespoons olive oil, divided

2 pork tenderloins (about 1 pound each)

12 green onions, ends trimmed

½ cup mayonnaise

1 canned chipotle pepper in adobo sauce, minced

2 teaspoons lime juice

12 dinner rolls, sliced in half horizontally

12 slices Monterey Jack cheese

1. Prepare grill for direct cooking over medium heat. Lightly oil grid.

2. Combine chili powder, cumin, salt and black pepper in small bowl; stir to blend. Rub 1 tablespoon oil evenly over pork. Sprinkle cumin mixture evenly over tenderloins; turn to coat. Place green onions and remaining 1 tablespoon oil in large resealable food storage bag; seal bag. Knead to coat green onions with oil.

3. Combine mayonnaise, chipotle and lime juice in small bowl; stir to blend. Cover and refrigerate.

4. Grill pork, covered, 15 minutes or until 160°F, turning occasionally. Remove to large cutting board. Tent with foil; let stand 10 minutes.

5. Meanwhile, grill green onions 3 minutes or until browned, turning frequently.

6. Coarsely chop green onions. Thinly slice pork. Evenly spread chipotle mayonnaise on bottom halves of rolls. Top with green onions, tenderloin slices and cheese. Replace roll tops. Serve immediately.

GRILLED PORK IN PITA
MAKES 6 SERVINGS

¾ cup Pace® Picante Sauce

½ cup plain yogurt

1 teaspoon lime juice

¼ teaspoon garlic powder **or** 2 cloves garlic, minced

1 pound boneless pork chops, ¾-inch thick

6 pita breads (6-inch), warmed

1 cup shredded lettuce

1 medium green onion, sliced (about 2 tablespoons)

1. Stir **3 tablespoons** picante sauce, yogurt and lime juice in a small bowl. Cover and refrigerate until ready to serve. Stir the remaining picante sauce and garlic powder in a small bowl.

2. Lightly oil the grill rack and heat the grill to medium-high. Grill the pork for 15 minutes or until it's cooked through, turning and brushing often with the picante sauce mixture. Discard any remaining picante sauce mixture.

3. Slice the pork into thin strips. Divide the pork among the pita breads. Top with the yogurt mixture, lettuce and green onion. Fold the pitas around the filling.

KITCHEN TIP

To warm the pita breads, wrap them in a plain paper towel. Microwave on HIGH for 1 minute or until they're warm.

PORK CHOPS WITH LAGER BARBECUE SAUCE

MAKES 4 SERVINGS

1 **cup lager**

⅓ **cup maple syrup**

3 **tablespoons molasses**

1 **teaspoon Mexican-style hot chili powder**

4 **bone-in, center-cut pork chops, 1 inch thick (2 to 2¼ pounds)**

Lager Barbecue Sauce (recipe follows)

¾ **teaspoon salt**

¼ **teaspoon black pepper**

1. Combine lager, maple syrup, molasses, chili powder and pork chops in large resealable food storage bag. Marinate in refrigerator 2 hours, turning occasionally. Prepare Lager Barbecue Sauce.

2. Prepare grill for direct cooking over medium-high heat. Lightly oil grid.

3. Remove pork chops from marinade; discard marinade. Sprinkle with salt and pepper. Grill 6 to 7 minutes per side or until 160°F. Serve with Lager Barbecue Sauce.

LAGER BARBECUE SAUCE

MAKES ABOUT ½ CUP

½ **cup lager**

⅓ **cup ketchup**

3 **tablespoons maple syrup**

2 **tablespoons finely chopped onion**

1 **tablespoon molasses**

1 **tablespoon cider vinegar**

½ **teaspoon Mexican-style hot chili powder**

Combine lager, ketchup, maple syrup, onion, molasses, vinegar and chili powder in small saucepan over medium heat. Bring to a simmer and cook, stirring occasionally, 10 to 12 minutes or until slightly thickened.

SOUTHWEST GRILLED PORK SALAD

MAKES 4 SERVINGS

½ cup mayonnaise

¼ cup orange juice

1 teaspoon grated orange peel

4 teaspoons chili powder

4 boneless pork chops

8 cups baby spinach leaves

2 oranges, cut into sections

1½ cups radishes, cut into matchsticks

1 cup FRENCH'S® French Fried Onions

Mix mayonnaise, juice and peel; reserve. Rub chili powder onto both sides of pork.

Grill pork over medium-high heat until no longer pink in center; cut into cubes.

Arrange spinach, oranges, radishes and pork on serving plates.

Serve with dressing and top with French Fried Onions.

BRATS WITH ONIONS & PEPPERS PACKET ▶

MAKES 6 SERVINGS

- 1 sheet (18×24-inch) REYNOLDS WRAP® Heavy Duty Foil
- 6 beef bratwurst sausages
- 1 small onion, thinly sliced
- ½ cup sweet and hot peppers, coarsely chopped
- 6 hot dog buns

PREHEAT grill to medium-high or oven to 450°F.

CENTER sausages on sheet of REYNOLDS WRAP® Heavy Duty Foil. Top with onion and peppers.

BRING up foil sides. Double fold top and ends to seal making one large foil packet, leaving room for heat circulation inside.

GRILL 15 to 20 minutes in covered grill **OR BAKE** 25 to 30 minutes on cookie sheet in oven. Serve on buns.

MEXICAN PORK CHOP PACKETS

MAKES 4 SERVINGS

- 4 sheets (12×18 inches each) REYNOLDS WRAP® Heavy Duty Foil
- 4 boneless pork chops, about ½ inch thick
- 1 teaspoon chili powder
- 1 cup chunky salsa
- 1 can (15¼-ounce) whole kernel corn, drained or 1 package (10-ounce) frozen whole kernel corn
- ½ cup chopped green bell pepper

PREHEAT grill to medium-high. Center 1 pork chop on each sheet of REYNOLDS WRAP® Heavy Duty Aluminum Foil; sprinkle evenly with chili powder. Spread salsa over pork chops. Top with vegetables.

BRING up foil sides. Double fold top and ends to seal packet, leaving room for heat circulation inside. Repeat to make 4 packets.

GRILL 10 to 12 minutes in covered grill.

PORK TENDERLOIN FAJITAS

MAKES 6 SERVINGS

1 pork tenderloin (about 1½ pounds)

1 packet (1.25 ounces) ORTEGA® Fajita Seasoning Mix

¾ cup water

2 tablespoons olive oil

1 red bell pepper, cut into thin strips

1 green bell pepper, cut into thin strips

1 onion, cut into thin strips

1 can (4 ounces) ORTEGA® Fire-Roasted Diced Green Chiles

Juice from ½ lime

12 (8-inch) ORTEGA® Flour Soft Tortillas

CUT pork down the middle lengthwise almost completely through, but not severed.

BLEND seasoning mix and water in shallow dish. Add pork and turn to coat. Cover and marinate 30 minutes in refrigerator.

HEAT oil in medium skillet over medium heat until hot. Add bell peppers and onion. Cook and stir 7 minutes or until tender and soft. Stir in chiles.

PREHEAT grill until piping hot, about 15 minutes. Grill pork 4 minutes on each side. Squeeze lime juice over pork and rest 5 minutes; slice pork thinly on bias.

WRAP tortillas in paper towels and microwave on HIGH (100% power) 1 minute. To assemble fajitas, wrap pork and vegetables in warm tortillas.

NOTE

This pork filling also can be used for tacos or as a topping on crunchy tortilla pizzas.

ASIAN-INSPIRED PORK & NECTARINE KABOBS

MAKES 4 SERVINGS

1 pork tenderloin
   (about 1 pound)
¾ cup pineapple juice
3 tablespoons soy sauce
1 tablespoon grated fresh
   ginger
1 teaspoon minced garlic
1 teaspoon ground cumin
1 teaspoon chili powder
½ teaspoon black pepper
3 fresh medium nectarines

1. Cut pork tenderloin in half lengthwise. Cut each half into eight pieces (16 pieces total). Place pork in large resealable food storage bag. Place bag in shallow dish.

2. Stir together pineapple juice, soy sauce, ginger, garlic, cumin, chili powder and pepper. Pour over pork; seal bag. Marinate in refrigerator 3 to 6 hours.

3. Prepare grill for direct cooking over medium heat. Lightly oil grid.

4. Cut each nectarine into eight chunks. Drain pork, discarding marinade. Thread pork and nectarine pieces onto eight short skewers. Grill kabobs 9 to 12 minutes or until pork is barely pink in center, turning once.

FRUITS & VEGETABLES

ROASTED SWEET POTATOES

MAKES 6 SERVINGS

6   sweet potatoes

Vegetable oil

Optional toppings:
mini marshmallows,
cinnamon, sugar and/
or butter

1. Prepare grill for direct cooking over medium heat. Rub each potato with oil. Place each potato on 6×6-inch piece of foil. Roll up to seal.

2. Grill potatoes 25 minutes or until potatoes are softened. Remove to heatproof surface using large tongs. Cool potatoes until cool enough to handle. Top as desired.

GRILLED ROMAINE HEARTS WITH TANGY VINAIGRETTE

MAKES 6 SERVINGS, PLUS 1 QUART VINAIGRETTE

TANGY VINAIGRETTE

- 3 cups cola beverage
- ⅓ cup white vinegar
- ⅓ cup canola oil
- ¼ cup sugar
- 1 teaspoon salt
- ½ teaspoon onion powder
- ½ teaspoon garlic powder
- 3 tablespoons ketchup
- 1 tablespoon balsamic vinegar
- ⅛ teaspoon black pepper
- 2 tablespoons honey mustard

ROMAINE HEARTS

- 6 romaine hearts
- ¼ to ½ cup olive oil
  Salt and black pepper

1. Combine cola, white vinegar, canola oil, sugar, 1 teaspoon salt, onion powder, garlic powder, ketchup, balsamic vinegar, ⅛ teaspoon pepper and mustard in medium bowl; set aside.

2. Prepare grill for direct cooking over medium heat. Lightly oil grid. Cut romaine hearts in half lengthwise; drizzle with olive oil and sprinkle generously with salt and pepper.

3. Grill about 2 minutes per side or until wilted and lightly charred. Drizzle with vinaigrette. Refrigerate remaining vinaigrette for another use.

PINEAPPLE WITH CARAMEL DIPPING SAUCE ▶

MAKES 4 SERVINGS

25 unwrapped caramels

⅓ cup half-and-half

¼ teaspoon rum flavoring

1 ripe pineapple, trimmed and cut into 8 (½-inch) slices

1. Prepare grill for direct cooking over medium heat. Lightly oil grid. Combine caramels, half-and-half and flavoring in small saucepan. Cook over low to medium-low heat, stirring until sauce is thick and smooth. Keep warm until ready to serve.

2. Grill pineapple 10 to 12 minutes or until pineapple softens and turns deeper yellow in color, turning once.

3. Place pineapple on large cutting board; cut into bite-size pieces. Discard core pieces. Serve pineapple with caramel sauce for dipping or drizzle over pineapple before serving.

LOADED GRILLED POTATO PACKET

MAKES 4 TO 6 SERVINGS

REYNOLDS WRAP® Non-Stick Foil

4 medium potatoes, cut into ½-inch cubes

1 large onion, diced

2 tablespoons olive oil

4 slices bacon, cooked and crumbled

2 teaspoons seasoned salt

1 tablespoon chopped fresh chives

1 cup shredded Cheddar cheese

Sour cream (optional)

PREHEAT grill to medium-high or oven to 450°F.

CENTER potatoes and onion on sheet of REYNOLDS WRAP® Non-Stick Foil with non-stick (dull) side toward food. Drizzle with olive oil. Sprinkle with crumbled bacon, seasoned salt, chives and cheese.

BRING up foil sides. Double fold top and ends to seal, making one large foil packet, leaving room for heat circulation inside.

GRILL 18 to 20 minutes in covered grill **OR BAKE** 30 to 35 minutes on a cookie sheet in oven. If desired, serve with sour cream.

GRILLED POTATO SALAD

MAKES 4 SERVINGS

¼ cup country-style Dijon mustard

2 tablespoons chopped fresh dill

1 tablespoon white wine vinegar or cider vinegar

1½ teaspoons salt, divided

¼ teaspoon black pepper

5 tablespoons olive oil, divided

8 cups water

2 pounds small red potatoes

1 green onion, thinly sliced

1. Prepare grill for direct cooking.

2. Whisk mustard, dill, vinegar, ½ teaspoon salt and pepper in measuring cup. Gradually whisk in 3 tablespoons oil. Set aside.

3. Bring water and remaining 1 teaspoon salt to a boil in large saucepan over medium-high heat. Cut potatoes into ½-inch slices. Add potatoes to saucepan; boil 5 minutes. Drain; return potatoes to saucepan. Drizzle with remaining 2 tablespoons oil; toss lightly.

4. Spray one side of large foil sheet with nonstick cooking spray. Transfer potatoes to foil; fold into packet. Place potato packet on grid. Grill 10 minutes or until potatoes are tender. Transfer potatoes to serving bowl. Sprinkle with green onion. Add dressing and toss gently to coat. Serve warm.

CHOCOLATE CAKE STUFFED ORANGES

MAKES 6 SERVINGS

6 large navel oranges

1 package (about 18 ounces) chocolate cake mix, plus ingredients to prepare mix

1. Slice ½ inch off top of stem end of each orange; reserve tops. Hollow out each orange, leaving ½ inch of flesh and peel around bottom and sides. Discard flesh or reserve for another use. Place each orange on 6×6-inch piece of foil sprayed with nonstick cooking spray.

2. Prepare grill for direct cooking over medium heat. Prepare cake mix according to package directions. Fill each orange two-thirds full with cake mix; replace tops of oranges. Roll foil up and around each orange to seal. Place oranges top side up on grill.

3. Grill oranges, covered, 1 hour or until toothpick inserted into centers comes out clean. Remove to heatproof surface using large tongs.

CAPRESE PORTOBELLO BURGERS ▶

MAKES 4 SERVINGS

- 3 ounces mozzarella cheese, diced
- 2 plum tomatoes, chopped
- 2 tablespoons chopped fresh basil
- 1 tablespoon balsamic vinaigrette
- 1 clove garlic, crushed
- ⅛ teaspoon black pepper
- 4 portobello mushrooms (about ¾ pound), gills and stems removed
- 4 whole wheat sandwich thin rounds, toasted

1. Prepare grill for direct cooking over medium-high heat. Lightly oil grid. Combine cheese, tomatoes, basil, vinaigrette, garlic and pepper in small bowl; toss to coat.

2. Grill mushroom caps, stem side down, 5 minutes on each side or until done. Spoon one fourth of tomato mixture into each cap. Cover and grill 3 minutes or until cheese is melted. Serve on sandwich thins.

NOTE

Cooked portobello mushrooms can be frozen and will keep for several months. Store in plastic containers or freezer bags.

ZUCCHINI & TOMATOES WITH FETA PACKET

MAKES 6 SERVINGS

- 1 sheet (18×24-inch) REYNOLDS WRAP® Heavy Duty Foil
- 3 medium zucchini, sliced
- 1 pint cherry tomatoes
- 2 teaspoons olive oil
- 1½ teaspoons dried Italian seasoning
- ½ teaspoon salt
- ¼ teaspoon black pepper
- ½ cup crumbled feta cheese

PREHEAT grill to medium-high or oven to 450°F.

COMBINE zucchini, tomatoes, olive oil, Italian seasoning, salt and pepper in a large bowl. Center mixture on sheet of REYNOLDS WRAP® Heavy Duty Foil.

BRING up foil sides. Double fold top and ends to form one large foil packet, leaving room for heat circulation inside.

GRILL 10 to 12 minutes in covered grill **OR BAKE** 15 to 20 minutes on cookie sheet in oven. Sprinkle with cheese before serving.

FIRE-ROASTED HASSELBACK POTATOES ▶

MAKES 6 SERVINGS

6 large baking potatoes
Olive oil
2 tablespoons garlic powder
1 tablespoon salt
2 teaspoons black pepper

1. Prepare grill for direct cooking over medium heat.

2. Cut each potato crosswise at ¼-inch-thick intervals, leaving about ¼ inch at bottom. Rub each potato with oil, garlic powder, salt and pepper, making sure oil and seasonings get inside potato slits. Place each potato on 6×6-inch piece of foil. Roll up to seal.

3. Grill potatoes, covered, 40 minutes or until potatoes are softened. Remove to heatproof surface using large tongs. Cool potatoes until cool enough to handle.

SOUTHERN SPICY GRILLED CORN

MAKES 4 SERVINGS

½ cup HELLMANN'S® or BEST FOODS® Real Mayonnaise
2 tablespoons chopped onion
1 tablespoon apple cider vinegar
½ tablespoon finely chopped garlic
½ teaspoon chipotle powder
4 ears corn-on-the-cob, halved

1. In small bowl, combine all ingredients except corn.

2. Grill corn, brushing frequently with mayonnaise mixture, until corn is tender. Garnish, if desired, with chopped fresh cilantro or parsley.

GRILLED SESAME ASPARAGUS

MAKES 4 SERVINGS

1 **pound medium asparagus spears (about 20), trimmed**

1 **tablespoon sesame seeds**

2 **to 3 teaspoons balsamic vinegar**

¼ **teaspoon salt**

¼ **teaspoon black pepper**

1. Prepare grill for direct cooking over medium heat. Lightly oil grid.

2. Place asparagus on baking sheet; spray lightly with nonstick cooking spray. Sprinkle with sesame seeds, rolling to coat.

3. Grill asparagus, uncovered, 4 to 6 minutes or until the asparagus begins to brown, turning once.

4. Remove asparagus to serving dish. Sprinkle with vinegar, salt and pepper.

TIP

Be sure to use the entire amount of pepper—it really brings out the flavors of this dish.

PEACHES WITH NUTMEG PASTRY CREAM

MAKES 4 SERVINGS

4 peaches, halved

2 tablespoons cinnamon-sugar*

3 egg yolks

⅓ cup sugar

2 tablespoons all-purpose flour

Pinch salt

1¼ cups whole milk

1 teaspoon vanilla

⅛ teaspoon ground nutmeg

2 tablespoons butter

Whipped cream (optional)

To make cinnamon-sugar, combine 2 tablespoons sugar with 1 teaspoon ground cinnamon in small bowl.

1. Prepare grill for direct cooking over medium-low heat. Sprinkle peach halves with cinnamon-sugar. Grill peaches just until tender and slightly golden brown. (Peaches should still be firm and hold shape.) Set aside.

2. Combine egg yolks, sugar, flour and salt in medium bowl; stir until well blended.

3. Bring milk, vanilla and nutmeg to a boil in medium saucepan over high heat. Whisking constantly, slowly add ¼ cup hot milk mixture to egg yolk mixture. Add egg yolk mixture to milk mixture in saucepan; cook, whisking constantly, until thickened. Remove from heat and add butter; whisk until well blended.

4. Spoon sauce onto dessert plates; arrange peach halves on top of sauce. Serve with whipped cream, if desired.

CORN ON THE COB WITH BUTTERY CITRUS SPREAD ▶

MAKES 4 SERVINGS

4 medium ears corn, husks and silks removed

2 tablespoons butter

1 tablespoon finely chopped parsley

1 teaspoon grated lemon peel

½ teaspoon black pepper

¼ teaspoon paprika

¼ teaspoon salt

1. Prepare grill for direct cooking over medium heat. Spray corn with nonstick cooking spray. Grill, covered, 18 to 20 minutes or until golden brown, turning frequently.

2. Meanwhile, combine butter, parsley, lemon peel, pepper, paprika and salt in small bowl; stir to blend. Serve corn with butter spread.

BARBECUE SEITAN SKEWERS

MAKES 4 SERVINGS

1 package (8 ounces) seitan, cubed

½ cup barbecue sauce, divided

1 red bell pepper, cut into 12 pieces

1 green bell pepper, cut into 12 pieces

12 cremini mushrooms

1 zucchini, cut into 12 pieces

1. Place seitan in medium bowl. Add ¼ cup barbecue sauce; stir to coat. Marinate in refrigerator 30 minutes. Soak four bamboo skewers in water 20 minutes.

2. Prepare grill for direct cooking over medium-high heat. Lightly oil grid. Thread seitan, bell peppers, mushrooms and zucchini onto skewers.

3. Grill skewers, covered, 8 minutes or until seitan is hot and glazed with sauce, brushing with remaining sauce and turning occasionally.

S'MORE BANANAS

MAKES 8 SERVINGS

8 bananas

24 mini marshmallows

8 tablespoons mini chocolate chips

8 tablespoons graham cracker crumbs

1. Prepare grill for direct cooking over medium heat.

2. Slice bananas lengthwise halfway through peel and flesh. Place each banana on 8×3-inch piece of foil. Place 3 marshmallows, 1 tablespoon chocolate chips and 1 tablespoon graham cracker crumbs in each banana slit. Roll up and seal foil around each banana.

3. Grill wrapped bananas, covered, 40 minutes. Remove to heatproof surface; let cool before handling.

CHOCOLATE-PEANUT BUTTER BANANAS

Substitute chocolate syrup, peanut butter and peanuts for the marshmallows, chocolate chips and graham cracker crumbs. Cook as directed above. Makes 8 servings.

SZECHUAN GRILLED MUSHROOMS

MAKES 4 SERVINGS

- 1 **pound large mushrooms**
- 2 **tablespoons soy sauce**
- 2 **teaspoons peanut or vegetable oil**
- 1 **teaspoon dark sesame oil**
- 1 **clove garlic, minced**
- ½ **teaspoon crushed Szechuan peppercorns or red pepper flakes**

1. Place mushrooms in large resealable food storage bag. Combine soy sauce, peanut oil, sesame oil, garlic and Szechuan peppercorns in small bowl; pour over mushrooms. Seal bag; turn to coat. Marinate at room temperature 15 minutes.

2. Prepare grill for direct cooking over medium heat. Lightly oil grid. Thread mushrooms onto skewers.*

3. Grill mushrooms 10 minutes or until lightly browned, turning once. Serve immediately.

If using wood skewers, soak in warm water 30 minutes to prevent burning.

VARIATION

For Szechuan Grilled Mushrooms and Onions, add 4 green onions, cut into 1½-inch pieces, to marinade. Alternately thread onto skewers with mushrooms. Proceed as directed in step 2.

PEACHES WITH SPICY CREAM CHEESE TOPPING

MAKES 6 SERVINGS

½ **cup (4 ounces) cream cheese, softened**

1 **tablespoon honey**

¼ **teaspoon ground red pepper**

2 **cups thawed frozen whipped topping**

6 **peaches, halved and pitted**

¼ **cup slivered almonds, toasted***

Fresh mint leaves (optional)

*To toast almonds, spread in single layer in heavy skillet. Cook and stir over medium heat 1 to 2 minutes or until nuts are lightly browned, stirring frequently.

1. Prepare grill for direct cooking over medium-high heat. Lightly oil grid.

2. Gently stir cream cheese in medium bowl until smooth. Whisk in honey and ground red pepper until well blended. Fold in whipped topping. Cover; refrigerate until ready to use.

3. Place peaches, cut sides down, on prepared grill. Grill, covered, 2 to 3 minutes. Turn. Grill 2 to 3 minutes or until peaches begin to soften. Remove to plate; let stand to cool slightly.

4. Arrange 2 peach halves, cut sides up, on six serving plates. Top evenly with spicy cream cheese topping and almonds. Garnish with mint.

JAMAICAN GRILLED SWEET POTATOES

MAKES 6 SERVINGS

- 2 large sweet potatoes or yams (about 1½ pounds)
- 3 tablespoons packed brown sugar
- 3 tablespoons melted butter, divided
- 1 teaspoon ground ginger
- 1 tablespoon chopped fresh cilantro
- 2 teaspoons dark rum

1. Pierce potatoes in several places with fork. Place on paper towel in microwave. Microwave on HIGH 5 to 6 minutes or until crisp-tender, rotating one-fourth turn halfway through cooking time. Let stand 10 minutes. Diagonally slice potatoes into ¾-inch slices.

2. Prepare grill for direct cooking over medium heat. Combine brown sugar, 1 tablespoon butter and ginger in small bowl; mix well. Stir in cilantro and rum; set aside. Lightly brush one side of each potato slice with half of remaining melted butter.

3. Grill sweet potato slices, butter side down, covered, 4 to 6 minutes or until grill marked. Brush tops with remaining melted butter. Turn. Grill 3 to 5 minutes or until grill marked. To serve, spoon rum mixture evenly over potato slices.

APPLES WITH BROWN SUGAR AND CINNAMON ▶

MAKES 4 SERVINGS

2 tablespoons packed brown sugar

1 tablespoon ground cinnamon

¼ teaspoon ground nutmeg

2 large apples (Red Delicious, Braeburn or Fuji), cored and sliced into 12 rings

Caramel or butterscotch sauce, warmed

Vanilla ice cream (optional)

1. Prepare grill for direct cooking over medium-low heat.

2. Combine brown sugar, cinnamon and nutmeg in small bowl; stir to blend. Sprinkle onto apple slices. Wrap apples in foil.

3. Grill apples 9 minutes or until tender and rich brown, but not mushy, turning as needed. Place on four plates and drizzle with caramel sauce. Add ice cream, if desired.

NOTE

A variety of fruit works great on the grill. Also try peaches wrapped in foil, sprinkled with brown sugar, cinnamon and butter. Grill 8 to 12 minutes until the fruit becomes soft.

HERB GRILLED VEGETABLES

MAKES 6 SERVINGS

¾ cup olive oil

¼ cup red wine vinegar

1 tablespoon lemon-pepper seasoning

2 cloves garlic, minced

1 medium eggplant (about 1¾ pounds), cut into ½-inch slices

2 medium zucchini, cut into ½-inch slices

Cherry tomatoes (optional)

1. Combine oil, vinegar, lemon-pepper seasoning and garlic in small bowl; mix well.

2. Place eggplant and zucchini in large bowl. Pour oil mixture over vegetables; turn to coat. Marinate 30 minutes.

3. Spray grill basket with nonstick cooking spray. Prepare grill for direct cooking over medium heat. Remove vegetables from marinade; reserve marinade. Grill vegetables, covered, over medium heat 8 to 16 minutes or until fork-tender, turning once or twice.

4. Return grilled vegetables and tomatoes, if desired, to large bowl; turn to coat with remaining marinade. Serve warm or at room temperature.

GRILLED FRUITS WITH ORANGE COUSCOUS

MAKES 4 SERVINGS

1⅓ cups quick-cooking couscous

½ teaspoon ground cinnamon

½ cup orange juice

2 tablespoons vegetable oil, divided

1 tablespoon soy sauce

1 tablespoon maple syrup

⅛ teaspoon ground nutmeg

½ cup raisins

½ cup chopped walnuts or pecans

2 ripe mangoes, quartered

½ fresh pineapple, cut into ½-inch slices

1. Prepare grill for direct cooking over medium heat. Lightly oil grid.

2. Prepare couscous according to package directions, adding cinnamon to water with couscous.

3. Meanwhile, blend orange juice, 1 tablespoon oil, soy sauce and maple syrup in glass measuring cup; set aside. Blend remaining 1 tablespoon oil and nutmeg in small bowl; set aside.

4. Cool couscous 5 minutes. Stir in orange juice mixture, raisins and walnuts. Transfer to serving bowl. Place bowl in center of large serving platter. Cover lightly.

5. Place mangoes, skin side down, and pineapple on prepared grid. Brush fruit with nutmeg mixture. Grill 5 to 7 minutes or until fruit soften, turning pineapple halfway through grilling time. Arrange grilled fruit around couscous on platter.

TIP

Purchase pineapple already trimmed and cored in produce refrigerated section or use cantaloupe wedges instead of mango.

Acknowledgments

The publisher would like to thank the companies and organizations listed below for the use of their recipes and photographs in this publication.

The Beef Checkoff
California Olive Committee
Campbell Soup Company
McCormick® & Compnay, Inc.
Ortega®, A Division of B&G Foods North America, Inc.
Pinnacle Foods
Recipes courtesy of the Reynolds Kitchens
Sargento® Foods Inc.
Unilever

VOLUME MEASUREMENTS (dry)

$1/8$ teaspoon = 0.5 mL
$1/4$ teaspoon = 1 mL
$1/2$ teaspoon = 2 mL
$3/4$ teaspoon = 4 mL
1 teaspoon = 5 mL
1 tablespoon = 15 mL
2 tablespoons = 30 mL
$1/4$ cup = 60 mL
$1/3$ cup = 75 mL
$1/2$ cup = 125 mL
$2/3$ cup = 150 mL
$3/4$ cup = 175 mL
1 cup = 250 mL
2 cups = 1 pint = 500 mL
3 cups = 750 mL
4 cups = 1 quart = 1 L

VOLUME MEASUREMENTS (fluid)

1 fluid ounce (2 tablespoons) = 30 mL
4 fluid ounces ($1/2$ cup) = 125 mL
8 fluid ounces (1 cup) = 250 mL
12 fluid ounces ($1 1/2$ cups) = 375 mL
16 fluid ounces (2 cups) = 500 mL

WEIGHTS (mass)

$1/2$ ounce = 15 g
1 ounce = 30 g
3 ounces = 90 g
4 ounces = 120 g
8 ounces = 225 g
10 ounces = 285 g
12 ounces = 360 g
16 ounces = 1 pound = 450 g

DIMENSIONS

$1/16$ inch = 2 mm
$1/8$ inch = 3 mm
$1/4$ inch = 6 mm
$1/2$ inch = 1.5 cm
$3/4$ inch = 2 cm
1 inch = 2.5 cm

OVEN TEMPERATURES

250°F = 120°C
275°F = 140°C
300°F = 150°C
325°F = 160°C
350°F = 180°C
375°F = 190°C
400°F = 200°C
425°F = 220°C
450°F = 230°C

BAKING PAN SIZES

Utensil	Size in Inches/Quarts	Metric Volume	Size in Centimeters
Baking or Cake Pan (square or rectangular)	8×8×2	2 L	20×20×5
	9×9×2	2.5 L	23×23×5
	12×8×2	3 L	30×20×5
	13×9×2	3.5 L	33×23×5
Loaf Pan	8×4×3	1.5 L	20×10×7
	9×5×3	2 L	23×13×7
Round Layer Cake Pan	8×1½	1.2 L	20×4
	9×1½	1.5 L	23×4
Pie Plate	8×1¼	750 mL	20×3
	9×1¼	1 L	23×3
Baking Dish or Casserole	1 quart	1 L	—
	1½ quart	1.5 L	—
	2 quart	2 L	—